My Leash on Life

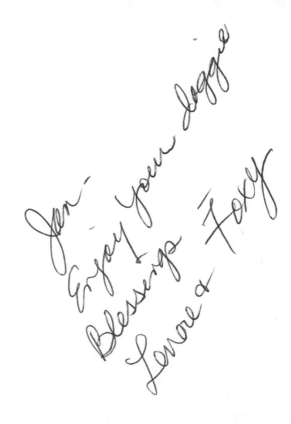

Jen ~
Enjoy your doggie
Blessings Foxy
Lenore &

MY LEASH ON LIFE

Foxy's View of the World from a Foot Off the Ground

LENORE HIRSCH

LAUGHING OAK
NAPA CALIFORNIA

FIRST EDITION
November 2013
Laughing Oak • Napa CA
www.myleashonlife.me

❧

ISBN: 978-0-6158726-5-0
Library of Congress Control Number:
2013916320

❧

Design, typography, and pre-press production:
Fearless Literary Services • *www.fearlessbooks.com*

Table of Contents

for Jay, who wanted a cat

"To me, you are still nothing more than a little boy who is just like a hundred thousand other little boys. And I have no need of you. And you, on your part, have no need of me. To you, I am nothing more than a fox like a hundred thousand other foxes. But if you tame me, then we shall need each other. To me, you will be unique in all the world. To you, I shall be unique in all the world..."

— THE LITTLE PRINCE, Antoine de Saint Exupéry

INTRODUCTION

D OGS LOVE our humans. There's no doubt about that. Even when we take off for an adventure, we return to your arms, our food bowls, and the comforting smells of home. You two-legs take care of us, but you have a lot to learn about dogs. Sometimes we follow you around hoping for a treat or a pat on the back and you ignore us. When we want to go out, we look you in the eye, we dance circles around you, and some of us even whine, but too often you look back like it's a complete mystery.

A few of you know how to fix us when we swallow a rock. You tell our people what to do when we pee in their shoes or cower under the bed. Some humans know how to get us to do tricks—*easy, get treats!* The dog whisperer works magic with scared dogs by acting like a dog himself. But it's hard to find advice from a dog.

So I decided to write this book. Yeah, I know, my paws don't even know how to hold a pencil, never mind work a keyboard. For a long time I didn't know what a book was. I just watched my human, Ellie, stretched out on the sofa, staring at piles of paper and turning a page once in a while. When she started telling me a story while looking at the book, I began to realize there's interesting stuff in books.

Ellie helped me write this book in order to tell you about my life. She put my story into words that people can understand. You'll probably be surprised at how much I know about you humans, just from watching, listening, and smelling. I know when you're worried or sad. I know when you're angry. Even if you don't yell or throw a plate across the room, you have a different scent. I know when you're going out in the car—*can I come too?* And when you go without me, I know where you've been by sniffing your shoes.

But I don't understand everything. And for those of you who told Ellie this book should show dogs talking to each other, please! We don't have conversations. Our communications are pretty simple: *Yes! Mine! I'm tough. Hey, cutie!* You get the idea.

No dog can buy this book, so two-legs, please take it home and read it with your favorite canine. The cats in the house probably won't be interested, but your special dog will curl up with you and help you to appreciate a story that he wishes he had written himself.

ONE

Spring

M Y EARLIEST memories are of a damp cardboard box on the back porch of a ranch house. My four-leg mom licked me until I was alert enough to take my first steps. I couldn't see much, but the air was warm and full of sweet smells. I heard chirping and felt shadows pass overhead. I sniffed my way to my mother's warm belly and joined the other pups in finding my first meal.

The door to the house banged open and closed and I heard people coming and going. Sometimes they picked me up and held me in their huge hands. They smelled so different from us dogs. I licked their salty hands and wanted more.

One by one, the other pups disappeared, but I stayed. As I grew, I got to know the humans who lived in the house: a man, a woman and two human pups, a boy and a girl. I spent my days eating, sleeping, and nosing into all corners of the house to discover its smells, sounds, and tastes. I especially liked hanging out in the food room, where the lady called Mom spent a lot of time. I was always on alert in this room, because food might fall on the floor, and I could sometimes snatch it before anyone noticed.

I love being out in the yard on a spring day. When flowers are growing everywhere I can sniff them from up close or on the breeze from far away. Some are sweet and some are bitter. They leave dust on my nose that makes me sneeze. Flying, buzzing creatures hang around the blossoms. I snap at them, but they're too fast for me and they always escape into the air. Flower scents blend together with pee on the lower leaves into a lovely fragrance. I'd like to be able to reach the tallest flowers, but have to settle for those close to me.

That first yard was wondrous, but there was so much more to explore in the world outside my familiar fence. Going for a walk was the highlight of my day. I never knew what I might find in the neighborhood—perhaps a friendly dog out for his afternoon exercise, an angry brute barking from his yard, or even some spilled food on the sidewalk. *French fries, yummy!*

TWO

A New Home

YOU DON'T have to ask me twice to go for a drive. "Ride" or "car" is all I need to hear and I'm out the door, ready to jump in. One day Mom put a basket of food in the back of the car, out of reach. It smelled like fish and chocolate chip cookies. *Tuna? Yum!* I wagged my tail in anticipation of a feast.

After a long drive, we entered a park with rolling hills and leafy trees. Dad carried the food basket to a shaded area near a big tree and Mom put down a blanket and spread out the food. Everyone sat and ate sandwiches and cookies. I knew they wouldn't offer me any, but when they got up to play a game with a ball and a stick, I licked all the crumbs off the blanket.

I snuck off to check out some bushes that smelled like pee and licorice. The pee route led me up a dirt trail, and I followed it, leaving my scented calling card here and there. Then I heard a loud crunching sound — maybe dry branches being trampled by another animal. I stopped very still and sniffed the air—definitely a creature with four legs. Peering into the trees, I saw something move. I took pursuit. I chased the little guy as he scampered away, until he scooted up a tree. He looked down at me and chattered away, as if to say, "Can't get me here!" I heard some big birds cawing and flying from tree to tree.

Then it happened. I heard rocks and sticks and leaves moving—crinkle, crunch, crash. A big rock came rolling down the hillside and was on top of me before I could react. I lost my footing and rolled down the hill. My back legs caught in some branches. *Ouch!*

I tried to get up, but couldn't. I licked the salty wetness off my leg. That made me feel a little better. I heard other animals in the woods. I couldn't get up, so I tried crawling. *Owww.*

The next thing I knew, darkness was all around me. I crawled under some leaves and fell asleep. I dreamed that a big mean dog was gnawing on my legs while my family called my name: "Peanut, Peanut, where are you?" When daylight came, I started crawling again.

I smelled something smoky and crawled toward it. *Bacon?* I heard a human laugh. A young boy approached slowly until he stood right in front of me. His face looked curious.

"Hey, little dog. Are you OK?"

At first I turned my head away from his face, but then I sniffed and licked the hand he held out. It smelled like tree sap and motor grease. He picked me up gently and carried me into a house. Inside I sniffed a mixture of trees, bacon, grease, burning wood, old coffee grounds, and rotting vegetables. *Yum! I'm hungry!*

The boy opened the cupboards and took out a box. It looked like what my boy and girl ate every morning. They never shared with me, but this boy opened the box, poured some in a bowl, and put it on the floor. *Not as crunchy as kibble. Kind of sweet.* I ate it all. Then he picked me up and put me in a sink with crusty dishes. He held my sore legs under the cold water. He dried me off with a towel and set me down on the floor. I shook and watched him turn on the noisy box with flashing lights.

I woke with a start. I heard engine noises outside. The light from the window was growing dim — soon it would be dark again. The front door banged open and a large man burst into the house, smelling of tobacco, sweat, and the woods.

He took one look at me and yelled, "Junior, what the hell is this goddamn dog doing here?"

Junior looked at the big guy and even though I detected his uneasiness, he answered sounding very bossy.

"I found him, Dad. He was hurt and hungry."

The man listened, but then he looked at me and

started to move. I smelled his anger and scurried as fast as I could with my sore legs and hid under a table. I crouched as low as I could get, and when he came closer, I scooted into a corner behind a pile of wood.

"Dammit," he yelled.

He backed away into another part of the house. I stayed behind the wood, appreciating its musty smell until he came back out.

"You can't keep that goddamn dog. Get rid of him," he ordered, and went outside. I heard car noises again and then silence. After a while, I crept out and went over to where Junior sat, giving off a tense and worried scent. He reached out to pet me and I let him. After a while, he turned the noise off and picked me up. He carried me to another room and put me on the sleeping platform. He shut the door. I hoped that would keep the big guy away. We both slept until sun-up.

That night I dreamed about all of the smells of my home. I remembered the sweet, tobacco smell from the room Dad spent so much time in, staring at a box of lights on his desk and puffing smoke around the room from a stick in his mouth. In my dream the big can in the food room swung open and closed, open and closed, over and over, teasing me with smells of discarded food and wrappings. *Yummy!* In real life, I had tried repeatedly to get into it, but one day the whole thing tipped over and crashed, sending me running for cover.

I dreamed about the clothing that Mom collected from everyone and took to the garage. She brought it back in a basket all warm and smelling sweet and sunny. If I had the opportunity, I'd take some pieces out, sniff them and roll on them to fully enjoy their scent. I was rolling around on them in my dream when Junior jumped out of the bed and woke me up.

The big guy had already left. Junior gave me more food from the box. I found a greasy spot on the floor and licked it. Junior let me out to do my morning routine. Fresh dew coated the grass. I licked the sweet blades and sniffed where other animals had been during the night. Junior threw a ball to me, close enough so I wouldn't have to run. I looked around and sniffed the ground, wondering if I could find my way home. My legs still hurt, so I followed Junior back inside.

Later that day, Junior and I sat outside in front of the house in the afternoon sun. I heard the truck long before Junior noticed. The man was back. He bounced out of the truck and stood with his legs apart, planted like trees. I had no time to hide. Junior rose with his hands on his hips.

The man yelled, "I told you to get rid of that god-damn dog. Am I going to have to do it myself? You're lucky I don't throw you out too!"

I crouched behind Junior's legs. The man pushed him aside easily and kicked at me. I moved, but not fast enough. His foot collided with my stomach and sent me flying. I landed with a dull thud.

I whined, "Waaaooo!" I tried to get away, but he kept coming after me, kicking. Behind me, Junior was breathing fast, yelling and crying.

"Please, Dad, I promise I'll get rid of him! Don't hurt him!"

The monster turned around and I slid under a bush. I couldn't see much, but I heard them yelling and then I heard a thump and Junior cried out.

"Owww! I'll do it. I'll do it."

I kept as still as possible and stayed under the bush. The door to the house slammed shut. I was hungry, but I stayed put. After a long time, I sensed darkness and felt cool air around me. Listening for noises, I crawled out, gave myself a good shake and looked around for something to eat—maybe an old bone. *Now a steak would be nice!* No luck. I hung around in the yard until sun-up. Then the door creaked open, I moved back into the trees, and the big guy left the house and departed in his truck. I approached slowly, hoping for food. Junior came out and saw me. He was limping.

"Little pup, I'm sorry, pal. You're going to have to go. I hope you'll be OK."

I didn't understand the words, but I knew that the man had won the fight. Junior's face was wet and tight as he chased me away. I knew he wasn't playing. I watched from a distance as he went back in and shut the door. My legs still hurt, but I knew I couldn't stay. I limped into the woods and didn't look back.

I headed toward the park and followed the road out to the highway. Cars passed me and then one stopped. I considered running away, but I didn't know how to get home. Instead, I perked up my ears, licked my snout and hoped for the best. A lady got out and talked in a soft voice.

"Don't be afraid, little guy. Are you lost?"

Well, yeah, lost, wounded, abused. Do you have any food?

I tilted my head and wagged my tail. She smelled of soap and coffee. She came closer. I sat and gave her my full attention, ears straight up. She smiled, grabbed my collar firmly and talked to another person in the car.

"No tags," she said. Then she picked me up and put me inside.

I sure hope there's food where we're going!

The car stopped at a big building. The lady carried me inside. When she opened the door, I could smell other animals and I heard barking. She put me down on a cold counter and, after a man behind the counter took my collar, she turned around and left. *Huh?* Ears back, tail between my legs, I tried to make myself very small. Would I ever find my way home?

THREE

Sniffing 101

YOU PROBABLY have noticed that my sense of smell is really important to me. I'll get back to the shelter in a few pages, but first I want to educate you on just how special sniffing is to a dog.

For humans, a walk or a run in the park is just about the dog "going potty." When it's cold or raining, people want to get out and back into the house as fast as possible. They don't understand how important sniffing is to us canines. Smells tell a story about everything in the world. I learn so much more by sniffing than by looking or listening.

Let's imagine you are out for your first walk in a new park. You come to a bush with buds and leaves hanging right at sniffer level. You sniff once. Mmmmm—scents of old pee, from more than one dog. You sniff again— a creature with wings has perched here. There's something floral going on, but very slight—the blossoms haven't opened yet. Because it's morning, the leaves are sprinkled with drops of dew, adding a sweetness to the bitter tang of the leaves. All of that is going on at once, so it takes a while to sniff it out.

My snout routinely identifies many different scents, like earthy, flowery, musky, salty, woody, sour, and sweaty. Pee and poop odors are a lot like food—like fish, grass, or meat.

To tease out each scent from this complex blend, I use the following method: First I sniff around the area from a few inches away, with short, shallow sniffs— nothing too intense. This gives me the combination of everything that's there. Then I move in and sniff more deeply, focusing on one fragrance at a time. If it smells especially interesting or food-like, I may take a lick. Often I decide to leave my own scent on the spot, so I pee a little. Sometimes I want to take the smell of the grass with me, so I lie down and roll on it. Once I've enjoyed every detail of the area's banquet of scents, I move on. If I'm walking with my nose down in the grass, I sniff so many times and so deeply that the air flowing out of my nose makes a soft snorting noise.

Dog parks are especially challenging places for sniffing. A community of dogs leaves unique scents all over the park. When I walk in, all of those tasty smells call, "Check me out," so I have to run back and forth and around in circles to catch them all. They tell the history of who has been there and when. Add to that the scents being given off by the dogs and people who are actually present. I pay careful attention to who is friendly and who is not, so that I can get away from any dog who may want to take a bite out of me.

Meeting and greeting is a special part of being at the dog park and involves exchanging sniffs of our hind parts. It is the very basis of dog manners. It can be difficult if the other dog is a lot bigger or smaller than I am. Then we can't sniff each other at the same time, but have to take turns. I have to get up on my hind legs to sniff some of the really big dogs. Please note that some dogs try this technique on humans, thrusting their noses into the human's crotch. I think this is gross, but maybe I'm just too short to appreciate the possibilities. (I do enjoy chewing up the underwear I find on the floor.)

Houses have nooks and crannies galore, with smells of all kinds—dust, mold, wax—hundreds of smells blended together into the smell of "home." In my house, each room has a basket that humans fill with all sorts of things: cans, scraps of food, pieces of metal, paper and plastic. When I'm alone, I like to check the baskets all over the house and see what smelly things I can find. My favorite is the soft papers that people use when they sneeze. I pluck them from the basket and play with them.

Then someone picks up the mess and puts it back into the basket, where I can find it again. When the basket is full, it gets emptied and starts to collect things all over again. This is an amusing indoor game for dogs and people.

In the late afternoon, I am usually snoozing on the sleeping platform upstairs when my humans start preparing food downstairs. Aromas of meat or fish and cooking vegetables travel up the stairway and gently stir me awake.

I know I am not likely to get any human food, but I still go down and check it out. I hang around while they eat dinner, in case anything falls, or someone decides to give me a little taste. When the humans are finished, I go over to my dish with its familiar kibble and chow down. At the end of the day, when I snuggle up in my bed, ready to drift off into dreams full of the scents of the day, I'm glad that I can enjoy all of the beautiful smells that make up the world. *I love my sniffer!*

I'd like to continue to congratulate myself on my nasal abilities, but it's time to go back to me shaking on the table at the shelter.

FOUR

No Shelter from Fear

A MAN in the huge building forced me into a cage that was just large enough for me to stand in. All day I crouched and shivered in the cage, yawning and licking my snout. My nose twitched, picking up anxious smells from the other animals. I had never been in such a small space. *Aooooow!*

I looked around at the other dogs in their cages. They growled, whimpered, or barked whenever the humans came by. After a while a man took me out of the cage, carried me to a room and put me on a cold table that was so shiny, I could see my head with its pointy nose, ears tucked and trembling, looking back at me. A different man with a shiny thing hanging around his neck talked softly. His coat smelled like fear. He put his hands on me. I turned my head away, my ears and tail drooping.

Don't touch me!

"You look like you've been through a lot. But

everything is OK now."

Hey, I know what "OK" means, but I don't believe you!

He felt my sore legs and my tummy where I had been kicked. He stuck something sharp into me. *Oww!* I tried to get away, but he held me so I couldn't move. He called out to someone, "Margie?" A woman came in and carried me to another room and put me into a sink. I didn't know what was happening, so I tried to crawl out, scraping my claws on the sides. By the time Margie lifted me out of the sink, we were both dripping wet. She dried me with a hot, noisy wind machine and put me back in my cage, which now had something soft on the bottom.

Margie smelled sweet like roses. Her head was covered with short curly hair like a poodle's and her hands felt soft and warm. Her face looked friendly.

She gave me one bowl with water and another with some kibble. *That's more like it.* I ate a little and fell asleep.

A loud chorus of barking woke me. Margie was back. She and a couple of men unlocked a group of us, put us on leashes and walked us outside. I didn't like the leash much, but it was good to get outside. Margie's feet moved quickly, "clomp, clomp, clomp." I sniffed in the direction of the other dogs. Margie stopped to let me pee and then pulled me to a new room that smelled like chicken. *Chicken? I'm starved.* Margie left me with a lady who had toys and treats. She told me, "Sit."

That's easy! Chicken? Yum!

"Good boy! Now down."

OK, more chicken!

She continued giving me treats and acting like I'd won some contest when I did what she wanted.

"Good job, fella! All right!"

Margie took me back to my cage. Soon it was dark and I went to sleep, listening to other dogs whimpering and sighing. I woke up many times, wondering where I was. I dreamed about the man who had kicked me and about the boulder coming down the hill. I basked in the love of my family, who had been so good to me.

In the morning, after some food and another walk outside, they put me in a roomy cage where I could walk around. All day long, humans of all shapes and sizes walked by and looked in at me. Some of them talked.

"Hey there, Marcel."

Who's Marcel?

"Look, Mom, what's wrong with this one?"

"Such beautiful red hair! I bet he sheds."

"Look at his fluffy tail!"

"The sign says he's dachshund and sheltie. Is that a good combination?"

"Don't be afraid, little dog!"

I thought one of them might be the man who had hurt me. I didn't even sniff them, but stayed in the back of the cage as far away as possible. When they called to me, I turned away. This went on day after day. Everyone seemed to be calling me "Marcel," so when I heard it I looked up, but I didn't want them to pet me. I didn't want them to put the leash on me. As lonely as I felt, I didn't want anyone near me.

One day Margie took me to a different part of the building. I saw the man with the shiny rope around his neck. *Uh oh.* He poked me with something sharp and then everything went fuzzy. When I woke up, I couldn't feel my bottom. After a while, back in my pen, it started to hurt. I was too tired to lick myself. I slept a lot for the next few days, dreaming I was being chased by angry humans.

Every day people came and looked at me and talked. I crouched and shivered in the back of the pen. I got food and water and walks, but I kept my distance from everyone.

One day when they took me out, I was pleasantly surprised to be let off the leash. I dashed off at first, but discovered a fence all around the yard, so I couldn't escape. I checked out some of the other dogs in the yard. I was beginning to enjoy sniffing them, when a short-haired dog twice my size bared his teeth and tried to bite me. I squealed and ran. After what seemed like forever, Margie took me inside and reached out to pet me, but I backed away. Once again in my pen, I continued to hide from everyone.

Life went on like this for a long time. Mealtime was the high point of the day.

No hamburger? OK, I'll take kibble. I was beginning to look forward to Margie's visits. She came to see me every day and talked to me in a very calm voice. I let her put her warm, pudgy hands on me. She called me her "poor little boy" and "pretty boy." One day she came to get me as usual for my walk outside, but we kept going.

"Don't be afraid," she said. "I'm going to take you home with me."

I didn't know the meaning of all her words, but she made it sound like a fun outing. Margie put me into a car that smelled like her. Would she take me back to the scary guy? Or better, would she take me back to my own family? Margie stopped the car in front of a strange house. When she opened the door, I stayed put, so she picked me up, carried me inside, and set me down on a slippery floor. The house smelled like dogs and, sure enough, a dog came running up to meet me. I pulled away at first, but then decided to give it a try.

Hi, guy. Want to sniff me? He had long hair, some dark and some light, and a stump where his tail should have been. We sniffed each other and then he growled.

"Sammy, stop that!" said Margie, and he ran off. She let me off the leash, but I stayed with her, following her around for the rest of the day. I began to relax, enjoying the familiar smells of food and laundry and Margie. At bedtime I followed her into the sleeping room and she patted the bed.

"Come on, you can come up here."

That seemed like the safest place to me, so I accepted. The other dog was on a lower level of the house, down some dark stairs. In the morning, Margie put me outside in the yard, where I sniffed flowers and trees and barked at cats and squirrels. Sammy stayed inside. Margie left in the car, and I spent the day chasing flies and watching everything that was going on in the street and in the yard.

For a while this was my daily routine: play in the yard, spend the evening with Margie, sleep on her bed. I had another new name, "Rufus." Sometimes I played with Sammy, but not for long. When she left us both alone in the house, I kept my distance. This was the best place I had been for a while, so although I had little appetite and didn't dare turn my back on Sammy, I began to settle in. I didn't know it was all about to change again.

FIVE

Park Place

I ENJOYED my days in Margie's yard, but even the best yard isn't as exciting as a park. I've seen parks with lakes for ducks and parks with rides for people, but my favorite parks are for dogs. They must be for dogs, because, besides the human escorts, it's dogs you find there. No cats! Margie took me to a park near a field with horses. Behind a wooden fence, I smelled horses and hay and then I heard dogs barking. I met the barking dogs and ran around in the bark! Human words are so funny.

I'd be happy to stay in a dog park all day, even if there are no canines in attendance! Every dog leaves his own special scent. First I look for the fence and follow it all around, occasionally marking the weeds. *Here I am!* Being off leash is like being left home alone with lots of toys and food and dirty clothes on the floor. I can stop and smell whenever I want for as long as I want. I can run as fast as my feet will take me until I can't run anymore. *Joy!*

Parks have all different kinds of dogs: tiny and giant, fussy girls and friendly boys, and bruisers who boss everyone else around. We do our usual meet and greet end-to-end and then go our separate ways. Sometimes we sniff each other's mouths, just to check what tasty morsel might have been there last. The big brutes play really rough, chasing and jumping on each other. Not my style. I bow, crouch and play chase with some guys who are my size, but only if they keep their paws off me.

When I meet a dog I like—usually a girl smaller than me who smells friendly—I give her a salute, ears straight up with my tail sweeping the air from side to side. I sniff her behind and her mouth and invite her to chase me by jumping away and bowing low. I may pee a little for her to sniff how awesome I am. Or I follow her around and sniff her some more, but soon enough some other scent attracts my attention and I'm off.

One time I got up on my back legs to get a good sniff of a tall girl poodle. At first, she let me sniff, but then she suddenly turned and clamped her huge mouth on my flank. I yelped, *Sorry, sorry*, but she held on, not exactly biting me, but letting me know who was boss. My human chased her off, but I stayed away from girl poodles for a while after that.

Some dogs spend their time chasing balls. Not me! I have to be pretty bored to chase a ball. Animals and smells are more interesting than toys anytime! Then there are the diggers. They don't socialize, but just keep digging their holes. Go near them and they'll chase you away, as though they were digging up buried treasure. I sniff out holes where little rodents hide, but some dogs freeze into position over one of those holes and stay there, until their human grabs their collar and pulls them away.

I never use the bars, tunnels and ramps at the dog park, unless it's to sniff and pee on them. If people think we like to do tricks for our own amusement, they are mistaken. *Got treats? Then we'll talk.*

When I'm thirsty, I look for the water dishes that are in all dog parks. After dogs wash their paws in those dishes, the water has an earthy flavor. Once I was checking the fence and found a place I could crawl under, so I did. The humans started in.

"Oh, no. That one got out!"

"Come back!"

"Where's the owner?"

"Hey, your dog is escaping into the street!"

They were running around and acting crazy. They called me to go back in through the gate. No problem— I wasn't trying to run away; I just wanted to see if I could crawl under the fence.

Once in a while dogs fight at the park. It's usually the bruisers who start the fights, with an intense stare and a growl. Their people will be off in the shade sitting in a chair and yapping away, not even noticing what is going on, until some dog is wailing and a brave person gets in the middle and breaks it up. Those people are lucky to leave without a canine impression in their arm or leg. Soon it becomes a human brawl.

"You better watch that dog of yours!"

"He doesn't belong in a dog park, if he's going to fight!"

"Your dog started it!"

"Wanna say that to my face?"

My humans have always stayed away from fighting, but they do have to watch out for other problems. When the dogs run in a pack, they sometimes knock people down. It's not very pretty to see a human lying in the mud crying. I try to stay away from the pack and the rough ones and I run away when I see trouble coming.

Some parks have long trails climbing up into the forest. I huff and puff up and down hills, sniff the perfumed trees and hunt for forest critters. Once I saw a snake slither across the trail in front of me. I went to check him out, but my human yelled for me to "wait" and then he was gone. When we're on trails, I run like I'm after a pesky squirrel, just for the fun of it, until I'm called. Sometimes my people go ahead while I stop to sniff something, but they wait for me to catch up. Occasionally, I strike out on a new route and they call and call until I appear around the bend. *Adventure Dog!*

Running in the park makes me feel like I'm all dog, not the guy who wears a hot-dog costume on Halloween or a shiny cape when it's raining hard. I'm the wild one who hears the coyotes howl in the forest and goes on alert, who thinks of catching his supper instead of eating what comes out of a paper bag, and who is totally in tune with the smells and sounds of nature. I wish my imagined bravery carried over to my days without a real den of my own.

Where were we? Back in Margie's yard.

SIX

Another New Home

At home with Margie on a warm afternoon, I was on my belly in the shade of a leafy tree when a car stopped in front of the house. I perked up, ready to defend my turf, but it drove away. Just starting to relax, I heard it again. A man and a woman got out of the car and approached the gate. I barked and howled my loudest and Margie came to the door, shushed me and said hello to the strangers. They went inside and I followed, at a distance.

"This is Rufus," said Margie.

"He's just as cute as the picture on the Internet," the lady said. I sniffed her feet encased in those lace-up shoes with rubber on the bottom, the kind I love to play with. The man had the same kind of shoes.

"He is a cutie, but he's so timid the shelter couldn't find a home for him," said Margie.

Margie handed the lady something that smelled like

pork and she held out a big piece to me!

"Here, boy, just for you." I grabbed it from her hand and scooted out of the room. I watched and listened from close by. The visitors looked alike. They had legs covered with coarse cloth. Taller than Margie, they wore shiny things over their eyes. As they talked, their hair bounced. They were talking about me.

"He's very sweet, just really shy," said Margie.

The man asked, "Does he go out for walks?"

Margie put the leash on me, and we all went out, but it was the two strangers who followed me down the sidewalk. Margie stayed behind. I hadn't been out on the leash since leaving the shelter. I pulled and struggled to run ahead, crossing the sidewalk back and forth to explore this new territory. The strangers talked to me and to each other.

"Hey, sweetie, slow down." Was he talking to her or to me?

The lady said, "He's so cute, Jay, can we take him?" as her leashed arm whipped back and forth.

"I don't know, he's not very friendly and he's wild on the leash."

"That's just temporary. He needs training. And I really want him!"

I only got to pee a couple of times before they turned me around and we headed back to Margie's. Not much of a walk. The visitors left the leash on while they talked to Margie and then took me out to their car and opened the door. *Huh?* Ears up and tail down, I pulled back, trying to retreat to Margie's yard. The woman picked me up and put me in the rear seat with the man. He held me firmly on his lap while she went around to the driver's seat and started the car.

I squirmed a bit, avoiding his eyes, then started sniffing his arms and legs. He smelled like fresh-washed laundry from the dryer.

"How is he doing, honey?" said the lady.

"He's settling down a little, but he sure is nervous."

I swayed with the movement of the car. That baloney that I had swallowed in one gulp was rolling around inside me like a big lump.

Jay started, "Ellie, I think he's going to—"

I threw up all over him. *Oops!* He didn't let go, but a strange sound came out of his mouth: "Aagh."

She answered his yelp, "I can't stop yet, Jay!"

After a few minutes, she pulled over and we got out. Ellie took me for a walk and put some water into her hands for me to drink. I licked, then sighed and lay down on the ground. I was feeling much better. Jay went off somewhere and came back with a wet shirt and pants, not smelling as sweet as he had before. We climbed back into the car and continued the journey.

When the car turned off the road, I looked out the window and saw a parking lot with a roof. As soon as the door opened, I jumped out, still on the leash, shook all over, and stretched a little. They led me into a long, two-story building with many doors and windows.

"Welcome to your new home. Here's the kitchen and here's the bedroom." She kept talking. *Looks cozy, smells like turkey.*

"Ellie, shall we give him some food?" Jay asked.

Good idea!

"Not yet, just some water for now."

They took the leash off and let me wander all over the house, although Ellie followed me. There was soft stuff on all of the floors, not like Margie's, where they were hard and shiny. The sleeping room had a big bed in it. Another room had a lot of furniture, but no beds. A table and chairs sat next to a narrow food room and of course there was the room with the soft furniture and the machine that flashes light and makes ear-piercing noise.

Later I heard Ellie say to Jay in a loud voice, "Please turn off the *tee vee* !" I knew "off" meant you better not do something. When Jay picked up a small tool and the machine went silent and dark, I learned "TV."

Over the next few days, I stayed near Ellie. I was afraid of Jay, although he didn't yell like the man I had met in the woods. I was watching and waiting to see what would happen. Ellie took me out frequently on the leash. There was no fence, but the area behind the building was shaded by tall trees, and I heard rushing water nearby. The first night, I slept on the bed with them. Then a soft cushion appeared next to the bed and Ellie tried to get me to sleep there. Every night she put a treat on the cushion and cooed at me when I got in to retrieve it.

"That's my good boy! Good job."

I learned to like the familiar smell of my bed. When I let Ellie rub my tummy, I was reminded of good times long ago.

Shortly after I came to this home, Ellie put a new collar on me. It had some shiny wafers on it that jingled when I walked. With my collar on, I think I got stepped on less.

At first, if Ellie or Jay went out, the other stayed at home. One day both of them departed, leaving me by myself. I sat by the door and barked, to let them know they had left me behind. They came right back inside. This happened a few more times— every time I barked to tell them to come back, they did. Then one afternoon they changed their clothes, shut the windows and turned the lights off.

"Ellie, are you ready? We're going to be late," he said.

"Honey, I know it's our anniversary, but do you think it's safe to leave the dog? He still barks as soon as we close the door."

"We can't take him with us to the restaurant and we both need a break," Jay answered. "We'll come back in an hour."

"OK, I guess it will help him to be ready when I go back to school."

Then they were gone. I sat by the door and listened to the humming lights and machines in the house—no people. I barked non-stop, but they didn't come back. Maybe they hadn't heard me. I barked louder. I jumped on the door, hoping it would open, but doors aren't made for guys like me to open. I kept barking until my throat hurt and my thirst sent me panting for water. Someone yelled from far away and I heard sounds of pounding through the wall. I stood by the door and barked and barked and barked. Finally the sound of footsteps told me that someone was coming to the door. I smelled Ellie and heard her voice. They came inside, and I jumped up and wagged my tail and ran around them, but they didn't seem so happy.

"Do you think he's been barking the whole time?" said Jay.

"He's pretty out of breath," said Ellie. "I bet we're going to hear from the neighbors."

They continued leaving me alone every few days. Ellie put treats inside a rubber ball, and I knew whenever I saw her preparing it that they were going out. Once in a while I got so scared when they were gone, I pooped. Then I was doubly nervous when they came home. I hid in a corner while they discovered my mistake.

"When is this dog going to calm down?" Jay asked.

"He's doing better, honey. Just be patient," Ellie answered, cleaning up the floor. In time I wasn't as uneasy when they left. Sometimes I got so busy with the treats in the ball that I forgot I was alone. And they always came back.

My life finally settled into a routine. They had a new name for me. If I came to attention when I heard "Foxy," I might get a treat or a tummy rub. Every morning, Ellie walked me next to a road lined with shrubs and trees. I kept things current by peeing on the same spots every day. Ellie fed me and then she left and I spent the day with Jay.

He watched the TV or sat in front of another screen and moved his fingers on a board, mumbling to himself. If he had something to eat, he gave me a taste. *Popcorn? Toss it this way. Cherries? Not so sure.* Sometimes we took a nap, or we drove to the coffee shop, where I was on crumb patrol. Later in the day, he took me for a walk. Unlike Ellie, who wanted me to walk by her side, Jay always waited while I sniffed and peed as often as I wanted.

When Ellie came home, she gave each of us a hug, then installed herself in the kitchen, banging pots and pans and cooking up a cloud of many scents which spread throughout the house. *Those little curly fish—shrimp? Love it!* There was crunchy food in my bowl, but I hoped for something better. When the two of them sat down to eat, I positioned myself close to the table. *Beef? Tasty! Peas rolling off a fork? Incoming!*

Most evenings, we sat on the sofa in front of the TV. I felt all warm and tingly when I could sit in between my two humans, with one stroking my head and the other giving me a back massage. Life was beginning to have a comfortable pattern and I expected it to last forever. I did not yet understand that life changes all the time. To survive, you have to deal with new things—the good, the bad, and the absolutely terrible.

SEVEN

Starbarks

IF I COULD make a list of my favorite things, it would start with food. I pay close attention to what everyone is eating or drinking, but I only get my kibble twice a day. Unlike me, my humans seem to be feeding their faces all the time. When they return to the car after leaving me in some parking spot, I try to get close enough to smell their mouths; often, I find they've been eating meat or chocolate or some other yummy item, without bringing anything but the scent back for me.

Sometimes they stop for food and drink when we're out walking, and that's how I got to know Starbarks. The main attraction seems to be the hot steaming coffee they serve in paper cups. Ellie and Jay used to brew coffee at home and let it sit for hours, making the whole house smell like Starbarks. I've sniffed and tasted the cold remains from a cup left on the floor and found it to be bitter and unappealing. On our morning walks, we often stopped at the local coffee place. I'd wait with my leash tied to an outside table while they went in to get their food and drinks.

The first time Ellie tied me to the table and disappeared, I panicked. *What? Wait for me!* I tried to follow her into the shop, and the table fell over. Crash!

Heads turned. Shaken, my tail between my legs, I dragged the table with me toward the door. I'm sure the sound of iron on concrete was heard by all the people on the block and by dogs farther away. Ellie came running and didn't go back into the shop. The next time Ellie must have really wanted her coffee, because she tied me to the table, then walked into the shop backwards, while repeating "wait" and keeping her eyes on me. I cocked my head and watched to see if she was going to fall over something in the store. Before I knew it, she was back. After a few times practicing this, I knew she would be coming back with food, so I learned to wait without causing an accident.

When Jay and Ellie were together, one went inside for the coffee and one stayed with me. Then they sat at my table and drank their coffee and talked, as only humans can do, on and on and on. If they had crumbly food, my job was to be ready to lick up any bits that dropped on the ground. Some tables come with the crumbs already in place and, with enough leash, I clean the floor under the other tables too. As good as humans are with their hands, they sure drop a lot of stuff on the floor whenever they eat! *Pumpkin cake? Yum.*

Most mornings Jay took me to Starbarks after Ellie left for the day. He always had some folded up paper with him. He'd look at it and turn the pages, making crinkly sounds, and then look some more. Then he'd take a pencil out of his pocket and scribble things. He talked occasionally to other people who came by—about me. The visiting person, usually a lady, would bend down to let me sniff her hand and then start asking questions.

"What kind of dog is that? How old is she?"

Jay would sometimes remember the right answer, and sometimes not.

"He's dachshund and uh—sheltie—er no, corgi— I don't know—and it's a he."

I am pretty cute! Got any treats?

"What a darling dog," she would coo and then go inside to get coffee.

Starbarks rocks when there are several dogs there. The furniture and leashes get in the way of the typical meet and greet, but we try. Some dogs sit at their tables very quietly and pay no attention to me; some of them bark or whimper and want to meet me. Then the humans have to decide whether to manage a social encounter; usually they're too focused on their coffee, cake and conversation to bother with us canine crumb-gatherers.

I had learned how to handle coffee shops, but there were many more challenges to come.

EIGHT

Two Schools

SOON AFTER I moved into my new home, Ellie and Jay took me to a building that smelled like every size and breed of dog I had ever met. We went into a cave-like room with a hard, cold floor. A bunch of other dogs leashed to their humans stood around the edges of the room. Some squealed or panted. I sniffed the tense air. It felt like being at the shelter, except we were all together in one space. The people sat on chairs, next to their dogs. Jay put a rug down for me and Ellie had a pocketful of something that smelled like sausage. *Sausage? For me?* I sniffed her pocket and waited to see what would happen next.

A lady with a calm, no-nonsense voice was the leader. She spoke and then gave directions to her large hairy dog. The leader said, "Sit, Bruno. Now stay." She walked away from Bruno, who looked like he'd sit there forever if she wanted him to. Now our turn. I wagged my tail at

Ellie. She and the others said, "Sit." One dog barked. The dog next to him bolted to get away. One lady screamed, "Sit, sit, sit" at her dog. I sat down and took my treat. *Yummy! Can we do that again?* "Stay" was harder, because I wanted to check out what the other dogs were doing, but after a few tries I figured that I could wait for the treat and then look around the room.

Another night, it was time for "leave it." I shook my head and started panting when the leader put a bunch of toys and food on the floor. Ellie tried to block me from getting to them, while saying "leave it." She had lots of treats, but the biscuit and squeak toy on the floor beckoned and I pounced. Next, the leader held me at one end of the room—on the longest leash I'd ever seen—while Ellie walked far away. When Ellie called me, it took me a moment to see where she was and head in her direction. The other dogs watched, thinking "He'll never find her." But I ran to Ellie and got my treat, and all of the people clapped their hands. Whew! I could tell Ellie was just as relieved as I was.

That whole time, Jay sat on the chair and watched. He didn't seem to know what to do—sort of like me! The inside lessons were hard enough, but after several sessions, we went outside. The leader wanted us to do the same stuff we had done before, still on the leash, but I had other things on my mind. Ellie said "sit" and "stay," but I was busy sniffing a bush that had recently been marked by another dog. Even the treats couldn't get me to pay attention. Ellie talked to the teacher at the end of that class and we never went back.

* * *

ONE DAY Ellie took me with her when she left in the morning. We drove to a cluster of buildings on a grassy hill. We walked by rooms full of people, through a double door into a cool tile hall, and then into an office. Three ladies who didn't smell at all familiar jumped up from their seats.

"Well, look who's here!"

"Hey, Foxy, how are you?

Ellie took me away from the people into a room and closed the door. I explored while she sat at a desk and looked at papers. Besides the desk and a bookshelf, the room had a table with chairs. I scanned for crumbs, but didn't find any. A little boy came in and he and Ellie talked for a while. He had an angry scent, but it softened before he left.

I was pretty bored, until she put me back on the leash and we left the office to walk around the grounds. Every room was full of children! Those rooms smelled like old books, pencils, and dust. I heard the class leaders talking quietly as we passed each room. When a bell rang, the children ran out laughing and yelling. They threw balls to each other and took snacks out of their pockets. *Snacks? Can we go say hello?* I pulled on the leash, but Ellie kept me close and when the children wanted to meet me, she asked them to stay away.

"He's very shy, and a bit overwhelmed. Give him space, OK?"

We walked around watching the kids bounce balls and chase each other. Then another bell rang and they all disappeared back into their rooms.

Another time, we walked right into one of those rooms full of children. Kid-sized desks and chairs filled the room and the children sat and waited, like dogs in their kennels. The kids looked at me and Ellie answered their questions.

"What does he eat?"

"He eats kibble made of potato and venison."

"Can he do any tricks?"

"Not really. He can sit and stay pretty well."

She told me to sit. I sat at attention with my ears stretched straight up. Then I did "down" and stayed in place while Ellie walked away from me. The children clapped their hands and cheered. *Where's my treat?*

"Can we pet him?"

"You can put your hand out, and maybe he'll sniff it."

"Will he bite?" a girl asked.

"No. He's timid, but he won't bite."

I took a whiff of those hands. *Mmmm, you had peanut butter. And you smell like the bathroom.*

When I stayed close, they ran their hands down my back. Then we returned to the office and I took a nap while Ellie sat at her desk. At the end of the day I heard the yells and laughter of the children, mixed with the sounds and smells of cars coming and going. When the building was empty, we went home to Jay.

I liked this school just as much as the one with the dogs and the treats. I liked exploring new places with their new smells and new spots to pee on. I couldn't wait to see where we would go next.

NINE

Summer

During the warmest weather, no water drops from the sky—if there's any around, it's sitting in a bowl or a pool or it's coming out of sprinklers. The tall, stale grass in the dog park mysteriously disappears overnight. The wider trail provides new space for me to explore. It's like a magic conclusion to a treasure hunt, sniffing the dried up droppings that are revealed when the grass is cut. The funky smells remain.

Heat doesn't slow me down on my walks, but humans hurry to finish. When we get home from the park Ellie brushes me and checks my paws for burs and foxtails that catch in my fur or poke my skin. I'd rather not have her touch my feet and rump, but it's a relief when she pulls one of those sharp things out. Once we were in the park and something tickled my nose and made me sneeze over and over again. Off to see the doggie doctor. I'm not sure what he did, but when I woke up, my nose hurt, my behind was sore, and my claws were shorter!

When it's hot, we are up early for our first walk, and sometimes my last walk doesn't happen until it is dark, long after dinner time. Some evenings I'm already curled up in my bed, snoozing away, when she calls me to go out.

Once in a while we go to a park next to the river, where people sit on the ground in the dark and a few make loud music with horns and drums. I don't mind giving up sleep for those events, because there is always a picnic going on—my own favorite kind of entertainment. I sniff around as far as the leash allows to find some bread crumbs or a morsel of food dropped on the grass or the neighbor's blanket. *Chicken salad? Slurp.* The evening may end with booms and bangs and bright lights in the sky. The humans make satisfied noises, ooohing and aahhing like they're getting the best tummy rub of their lives, but I'd just as soon hide under a chair or someone's leg.

TEN

A Moving Experience

As soon as Ellie called for me to get into the car, I took off and in one leap, crash landed in the back seat. *Let's go!* Jay drove and Ellie rumpled a bunch of papers on her lap, holding them up in front of her face and staring at them intently. She talked like she was telling Jay to "sit" or "stay."

"Turn left, no, I mean turn right. OK, slow down."

We turned into a street I had never seen or smelled before. Jay drove slowly, while Ellie looked at the papers, out the window, and back at the papers again. Then she yelled, "Stop! This is it."

Through the window, I saw a house with its door standing open. They got out of the car, leaving a window cracked open. I sniffed in their direction, but didn't pick up a scent of danger, so I curled up for a nap. Soon they returned and we drove off, but Ellie continued to look at the papers and give directions, until we stopped at a second house. This time I tried to get out of the car, but they pushed me back in and closed the door, disappearing again. This continued until they finally let me out for a short walk. We were on a narrow street that ended at a fence with a big hill beyond it. The house we were parked by had a small lawn with a tall flowering tree that smelled sweet and shaded the lawn. The grass felt cool and damp on my feet and I picked up a whiff of other dogs. We walked around a corner to another narrow street with houses that looked just like the ones we had left, then returned to the car.

"What do you think, Jay?" asked Ellie.

"I think it's too expensive."

"I've got that all figured out. This is the one."

A few days later, Ellie and I drove back to the last house we had visited. A strange man met us there and this time I got to go inside. It was enormous, like a parking garage with no cars. I could see into every corner. Scents of people and animals lingered, but it would take some time to sort them out. My claws clicked on the tile floor. The humans' voices boomed in the stillness of the house.

"We need a three bedroom, and three bathrooms are a plus," she said. "The place we're living in now is just too small for all of our stuff, and we'll need a guest room, when Jay's brother comes."

"You'll love this neighborhood," he answered. "It's

quiet and close to shopping."

"That's great," Ellie said. "Jay needs to be able to get around on foot."

This place was bigger than our house by the creek, and like the first house I had lived in, it had stairs. I barreled up those stairs and sniffed every room. I remembered being a puppy and for the first time exploring the noises and smells that come from water rooms. I wondered what humans could possibly be doing in there for so long. And why they always closed the door so I couldn't find out.

The best part was the yard. We went out through a sliding glass door to a concrete floor, with dirt around the sides and a fence. It didn't wrap around the house like Margie's, but it had plants and trees. Birds chirped and I picked up an animal aroma on the breeze. Ellie and the man talked the whole time we were there and she scribbled on a piece of paper. Finally, we went home to Jay.

Soon after this visit, Ellie started a new project. Every day she brought some pieces of heavy paper into the house, made them into boxes, and filled them with our things. She taped each box closed and marked on the side with a stinky pen. Even my toys went into a box. *Hey! I need that ball!* Ellie stacked the boxes by the wall.

It was around this time that Jay began to change. Sometimes he didn't take me on my afternoon walk.

I tried to remind him by sitting by the door, or staring at him, but he didn't take notice. He spent more time sleeping and watching the TV. We still went out for long rides in the car, but he never stopped anywhere. We just drove around and then went home.

Jay and Ellie had taken me to visit other people and their dogs. We hiked with Mary and her boy dog Scruffy, who was about my size. Scruffy's hair hung down into his eyes. Mary always gave me treats and frequently had parties with a lot of people and food. Scruffy and I spent the evening chasing each other and then busied ourselves cleaning the floor. *Pretzel crumbs! Yum!*

Once in a while I stayed at Gretchen's house overnight. A very tall woman with a deep voice, she loved to cuddle with me. Her girl dog Shadow, with dark curly hair, constantly ran and jumped on everything, including me!

Hey, girlfriend, get off!

Gretchen's yard spread way up into the hills—when left outside Shadow and I became explorers.

When almost everything in the house had been put into a box, Ellie took me to Gretchen's house. Jay came to pick me up later in the day, but we didn't go home; we went to the house with the flowery tree. When he opened the door, I saw and smelled our furniture and Ellie's boxes had magically appeared! They let me run through every room and then put me out in the yard. *Yippee!* Ellie spent the next few days unpacking boxes, and Jay spent most of his time sitting in a chair.

It took me a few days to realize that we weren't going back to the house by the creek. I was sniffing a whole new neighborhood of smells on every walk. I discovered some big buildings on the other side of the hill. All day long, I heard bells and buzzers from that place. Sometimes at night loud music and yelling drifted over the hill. Early in the morning a herd of young people went streaming in, talking and laughing. They did the same in reverse in the afternoon. When we walked down the sidewalk nearby, I found yummy food wrappers (and an occasional beer can) in the bushes. When no people were there, Ellie took me running on the grass or the dirt track around the field.

The new house was full of activity. Strange people came in and moved things around. Bang! Clank! I jumped out of the way and watched them move the furniture out of the living room. They carried in wood and spent days pounding it onto the floor. Other people came and put stinky new cloth down on the upstairs floors. They spent a day putting some wet smelly stuff on the walls. Ellie seemed really pleased. I tried not to sniff. I wanted to go out into the little yard and lie in the shade of a sweet-smelling tree, rather than breathe the air in a noisy, stinky house.

My walks with Jay became slower and slower. He got

in and out of the car with Ellie's help. They drove often to a tall building, leaving me to wait in the car. When they returned, Ellie always took me for a walk, while Jay sat in the car. One day she opened the door and they sat down. No walk. Her face was wet and sadness seeped from her as they talked. Jay was quiet.

"Honey, I was ready to retire anyway. Let's do some traveling together and see how you do."

Jay said, "Are you sure?"

When we got home, they sat down on the couch and just stayed there holding hands and talking quietly for a long time. Something was wrong. She was ignoring me and he was hardly talking at all.

ELEVEN

Shepherd

I NEVER know what's in store for me when Ellie and Jay invite me into the car. It's a mystery until it's too late to hide under the bed. That's where I would rather have been on the day Ellie took me to the sheep ranch.

Now I've seen a few sheep in my day. Dr. Nick, who liked to stick needles in me, actually had one in a pen outside his office. Ellie tried to get me to notice it and sniff it. *Yeah, it's a sheep. Smells like your sweater. So?*

Jay was snoozing on the couch on a hot summer afternoon when Ellie announced a trip in the car. She brought along that box she wears around her neck that flashes and clicks. We drove for a while and then turned off the main road, followed a dusty lane and parked at a place where I smelled dogs, horses, and—you guessed it—sheep.

I could smell all of this but saw no living things, unless you counted the dry grass, trampled and still in the heat.

We walked around until an old sweaty man with hair on his face and a crumpled hat on his head came to see what we wanted.

"You're the one who called about the sheep herding?"

"I just want to find out if he has the instinct," Ellie answered.

"I'm Pete. Give me a minute to round them up. We'll be in that pen."

We stood there in the blazing heat. I looked around for some shade or a water bowl. Ellie shifted from foot to foot and wiped her face with her sleeve.

"A real cowboy, Foxy!"

Huh?

In a few minutes, Pete invited us into a fenced area. *Got water?*

Ellie led me into the pen and took off my leash. The sheep, dancing on their toes and avoiding my glance, were huddled on the other side of the round pen. I found a sliver of shade and sat down.

"Foxy, look at the sheep! Let's go get 'em!" Ellie yelled at me in a very excited way, as if those sheep were the most interesting things she'd ever seen. The cowboy stood with his hands on his hips. I looked at Ellie, then away. Still no water. *What do you want?*

Ellie started chasing the sheep, calling me. "Foxy, come on! Let's get 'em!"

She wanted me to follow her, I guess. But why? I moved out of the way as she chased the sheep around the curved fence toward me. The box hanging from her neck swayed from side to side. I walked to the other side of the pen.

Ellie's face was shiny with sweat. She stopped to catch her breath and propped her hands on her knees, head down. The sheep huddled away from her. I found my sliver of shade and sat down. Once again, she chased the sheep. They ran around the curve and forced me to move out of the way. Now Ellie was breathing hard. She opened the box and clicked at me and again at the sheep.

"Gosh, it's hot out here," she said, but Pete and I ignored her.

Pete announced, "I'll give you a few more minutes, Ma'am," and left.

Ellie looked at me. I looked down at the ground. "OK, Foxy," she said, "I guess you're not a shepherd after all." Finally we climbed back into the car and relaxed in the cool air until we got home.

The next morning, Ellie got out of bed early and dressed, leaving Jay to snore some more. She was sitting in a chair putting on her socks and shoes when I ran up to her like I always do before our walks. As usual, she held out a hand to pet me; I skidded to a stop and turned away, running and looking back to see if she was following. She was still fussing with her shoes, so I ran at her again, stopped short, nipped at her toes and turned away again. *Come on! Walk time!*

Ellie laughed and shook her head. "Foxy, I spent all that money to see if you can herd sheep and the only thing you're interested in herding is me!"

TWELVE

Sand and Water

RIGHT AFTER my visit to the ranch, Jay and Ellie took me on my first trip to the beach. They filled the car with blankets, coats, and a cooler of food.

Yes! Picnic!

While we drove, the air coming in my back window changed from warm and sunny to cool and foggy. The breeze filled my nose with fragrances of plants, fish, and salty water. It was like standing in front of the open refrigerator on a warm day. We walked on the sand down to the sea.

The sand felt soft and warm. My paws sank in and when I lifted each one, I sprayed sand behind me. *Cool!* As far as I could see, there was sand. Except for where there was water. Lots of water. More water than I had ever seen. Noisy water—whoosh...scrape, scrape, crash, whoosh... It never stopped. I tried to stay away from that water, even when Ellie wanted to pull me in. I was thirsty, so, after sniffing the shoreline, I took a tiny lick. *Ew!* It tasted like too many potato chips.

That first time, we only stayed long enough for a walk on the sand and a quick picnic. Since then I have been to the beach for a whole day and overnight. I love running on the sand. I can see the ocean and the shore, with nothing blocking my view. I run fast with no rocks or trees to slow me down. When the sand is hot, I'm happy if my people bring an umbrella and a blanket to make a shady spot for us.

The sand is constantly changing—sometimes it's wet and smells from tiny hidden creatures, alive and dead. The dry parts smell like dogs, insects, birds, and the rotten, rubbery plants that the water leaves behind. On my morning walk, the plants, shells and sand hills I marked the night before are gone. I have to get busy and pee on any new items that have appeared. I dig up shells and fishy creatures in the wet sand, but they crawl away from my sniffer. I consider eating them, but another smell calls me and I'm off to track it down. Once I found a deliciously stinky dead bird and had a great time rolling around on it, until Ellie shouted, "Leave it." Unfortunately, that's one of her favorite expressions.

Wonderful things happen to people when they stay at the beach. All the tense, tight scents they give out at home fade away and they become so relaxed, they don't yell or forget to walk me or feed me. We don't go out in the car for days and days. I get lots of snuggling and long walks on the sand, usually without a leash. I have to be careful not to get sand in my nose or mouth. That's why I refuse to chase a ball at the beach. Unless you like the crunch of sand in your teeth, I don't recommend it.

When there are dogs running free, I get to meet them and see who can run the fastest. I watch them run in and out of the water, chasing balls or sticks. *You're nuts, Bowser! You're soaked, just to get your stupid ball?* If people put down blankets for a picnic, I walk over to check out the food.

"Hey, cute doggie!"

Whatever they say to me, I'm more interested in their picnic basket. In fact, the best time to visit is when they've stepped away from their blanket and have left the basket without a guard. *Wowza, fried chicken!*

Of course, there's always Ellie with her blasted "leave it." We walk a lot longer on the sand than we do at home on the sidewalk, so I'm always tired and hungry at the end of a beach day. After a long walk near the water, I like to eat something, clean the sand out of my paws, and take a nap. Actually, that's what the people do too. Seaside time is relaxing for all of us.

The beach isn't the only place where I have to watch out for water. There is the routine of my bath, which happens in the kitchen at home. Ellie picks me up, takes off my collar, and puts me in the sink.

"OK Foxy, we're going to get you nice and clean!" As if she thinks that's something I would like! She uses a hose to spray water on me. Then she pours on some flowery shampoo and rubs. She keeps repeating, "Good boy, now wait, good boy, wait." She's trying to keep me from shaking while I'm still in close range. Finally, she washes it all off, wraps me in a towel and puts me down on the floor. I can't wait to get out of that towel and shake! Once released, I run around the house and try to spin the rest of the wetness off. If she lets me outside, I jump into the bushes and roll around. After a bath, it takes a while for me to start smelling like myself again, and soon it's bath time once more. That's life with humans.

Bath time is OK, but the backyard pool is another matter. My first time in a pool happened on a visit to a man and two dogs, Maggie and Harry, who live in the desert. Those dogs acted like they'd just been let out of a cage at the shelter. They had short fur with big spots. They were smaller than me, but sure let me know who was boss at their house—Maggie, the girl. They ran around in circles in their yard, barking, just for fun. At first I liked this game, but then I was ready for a rest. No such luck. Jay tossed balls for us to chase. He had to throw several balls, because, although Harry and I tried our best, Maggie insisted on getting the ball every time. So it was one for Foxy and Harry, one for Maggie, and so on.

The yard had a border of plants and trees and a big hole filled with water, which I learned is called a pool. Humans like to be in a pool when it is hot and it was really hot in the desert. Ellie spent a lot of time there, swimming around, splashing and talking to Jay and her friend. That was fine with me. I found a shady spot for a snooze.

One day while Ellie was in the pool, she called to me: "Come here, Foxy!" She wanted me to walk over to the edge. I could tell by the chuckle in her voice that she was up to no good, and that water smelled like medicine, so I stayed away. The next time she got out of the water, she said, "Sit," and being a good boy, I sat. Then she picked me up and walked right into the pool carrying me! She went down into the water and let me go!

Help! Tricked again.

My feet were moving like crazy, trying to grab onto something. I guess you could say I was swimming. I sure wanted out of that pool. Fortunately we were near the edge and I was able to climb out pretty fast. I have to admit the cool water felt good.

So when she got in the next time, I let her pick me up and take me back into the water. This time I had to swim farther to escape. Again I felt refreshed. We did this game every day. I bet she thought I would like the pool so much, I would jump in and swim around.

No way, José! Not me!

My girlfriend, Miss Fluffy, also has a pool in her yard. Sometimes Ellie or Miss Fluffy's human, Maria, carries me in. It's fun to play with them, but one thing that Miss Fluffy and I agree on completely is that we'd rather stay dry. We're just not water dogs.

My first trip with Jay and Ellie was to the beach, but there were many more outings that followed. There is nothing quite like peeing in a brand-new place.

THIRTEEN

Travels with Foxy

YOU HUMANS know what is going to happen when you get into a car; for a dog it's a mystery. It could be a short trip to some shopping center, where I am not allowed out of the car—boring! The drive could end at the doggie doctor, who will whisper sweet nothings while sticking needles in me. *Grrr.* I know an overnight trip is coming when my humans put my bed into the car.

Soon after we moved into our new house, Ellie packed some bags. My tail got to wagging when Jay carried my bed to the waiting car.

Road trip!

Ellie put my food and water dishes on the floor in the back and we were off. Jay drove. With my nose glued to the window, I saw so much speeding by: other cars, trees, dogs, and people. It's a challenge to balance on the seat while the car stops and starts up so often. Sometimes I find myself on my back on the floor.

The first time we stopped, Ellie took me for a short walk in a town with one block, a narrow sidewalk, and no people. I found some plants to pee on and picked up some other dogs' scents, but no four-legged critters were in sight. The second time we stopped, they left me in the car and went into a shop. They returned smelling like beef and potatoes. *Mmm…where's mine?* I listened to the road sounds and fell into a light sleep. We stopped at a long house with lots of doors right next to the parking area. They carried the bags through one of those doors and then brought me in.

We had just one room with two beds and a bathroom. The carpeting had many stories to tell. I followed scent trails all over the room and into the four corners. Then I checked under the beds to see if anyone had left a toy or a biscuit behind. No luck. Ellie put a sheet from home on top of one of the beds and invited me up for a snuggle. Jay turned on the noisy TV and the two of them cuddled up.

Ellie took me for a before-dinner walk up and down some nearby streets. We didn't see any other dogs and I was soon panting from the heat, but I enjoyed sniffing a new place and leaving my mark. When we got back to Jay, Ellie left by herself and returned with food in little boxes. I smelled fish before she came in the door. *Shrimp? Yes!* I licked my snout in anticipation. When I saw them eating it with sticks, I was hopeful that something would fall within reach, but I had to settle for my regular food. I slept in my bed and in the morning, after a quick walk, we were off again.

We drove for many days. Every day the two people I loved talked angrily to each other while I cowered in the back seat. Jay drove first. Then Ellie started complaining.

"Jay, you're driving too fast."

"No, I'm not."

"Jay, you're not staying in the lane!"

"I'm OK!"

Eventually, he pulled off the road. They sat and talked loud, like they were fighting over a bone. Then they got out and changed places. She drove the rest of the way.

On the second day, we stopped at a place with no buildings or people, not even any trees, just tall plants growing as far as I could see. Ellie and I went for a walk while Jay stayed in the car. I couldn't find any grass to sniff or pee on, so had to leave my scent on a few rocks and the hot, dusty ground. I sniffed close to one of the plants and something sharp pricked my nose. *Ouch!* It was a short stop.

I looked out the window at an endless landscape of small hills and prickly plants. Finally we came to a town and found a place to sleep. Ellie parked the car and Jay walked slowly to the room and went to bed while she carried in the bags and took me for a walk. That was our new way of doing things. Sometimes Jay woke up and they went out to eat, leaving me in the car. They didn't talk a lot in the evening. I usually jumped up between them and rolled over on my back. If I could get them to give me some love, their bad moods softened and everything felt much better.

One night we stayed in a city with tall buildings lit up by flashing lights. Cars honked and crowds of people filled the sidewalks. Out for a walk, I felt lost in a valley of concrete. I trotted over the blazing hot sidewalk, trying to make paw contact short. Ellie stopped to sit on a low wall next to the only grass in the area. As I was leaving a deposit, a bus stopped in front of us and the driver yelled and pointed at a sign next to me.

"Hey lady, it says *No dogs!*"

"I'm going to pick it up," she yelled back. "Where else is he supposed to go?"

We left early the next morning. I was starting to miss my usual daily routines—my walk around the block, the familiar dogs along the way, the dog park. This was the longest I had ever been away in a car.

The next time we stopped for a walk, it wasn't so hot or dusty. I didn't see any of those prickly plants but instead, some fragrant trees and flowers. The earth smelled very different—rich and metallic. They weren't arguing, so it was a pretty happy day. We stopped at a sleeping place in a quiet area. I saw no people. Jay went to sleep and didn't even wake up for dinner. Ellie took me for a walk down an empty street.

I smelled him long before I saw him. He had a bold, earthy smell. He stood as tall as a horse and his huge head was bent to the grass, munching. Funny bones were growing out of his head. I had seen one of these animals before, from inside our first home, at dusk. He had walked by near the creek and left before I could get a good sniff. This guy was just across the narrow road, and in bright daylight was enormous. My ears stood at attention, my tail wagged furiously.

Hey, buddy, want to sniff me?

He looked up at me and then lowered his head again. I sniffed and pulled at the leash to get closer. Ellie pulled back.

"Foxy, uh uh, that guy doesn't want to meet you!"

He turned and walked away. I shook all over and went back to sniffing the ground.

The next morning, I was eager to look for the local four-leg. I sniffed the chilly air, but found no trace of the guy we had met the night before. We drove into an area with a long, narrow parking lot, with slots full of cars. When we got out and walked around, I saw a rock wall and a fence. A crowd of people stood near the fence

69

looking out into space.

"Wow," said a lady, "what an amazing sight!"

"How'd you like to walk all the way down there?" asked a man.

Ellie and Jay just looked, holding hands. We were on a mountain with a valley far, far below us. All around us were rocks and more rocks and on the other side of the biggest valley I had ever seen, I thought I saw even more rocks. The air smelled fresh and clean. Any animals were too far away to identify. Ellie used her little dark flashing box, pointing it at the valley and the stone walls.

We went back to our room and everyone took a nap. Just before it was dark, we drove back to the parking area to look over the fence again. The air was cold. I would rather have been back in our room asleep, but a crowd of people stood at the edge looking out, their attention captured by what they saw. They reminded me of how hunting dogs, having found their prey, will stand and watch it all day until someone calls them off.

The next day, I was ready to go somewhere new. On our morning walk, we saw three of the creatures with the bones on their heads, too busy munching grass to pay attention to me. I wanted to sneak up on them for a good whiff, but Ellie wouldn't let me get close. Packed up and back on the road, we drove by fields of rocks, but no more deep valleys. When we opened the doors in front of a tall building, it was warm again.

I looked up into the sky at the hotel. I didn't see any stairs going up, even after we went inside. *Huh? How to get up there?* We walked into a tiny room with a door that slid shut. Then the whole room made a whirring noise and moved up. I learned the hard way how to get on and off the moving room—quickly. If you're poky, the door might bite off your tail! We walked down a long hall with many doors. I had to be careful, since Ellie was pulling a rolling suitcase with another bag bouncing on top. I was ready to jump out of the way if something dropped. Food smells trickled under some doors, and crusty dishes on the floor by others called to me. Even though she was busy with the bags, Ellie kept me from checking them out.

When we got to our room, Jay went to sleep, but instead of hanging out, Ellie took me in the car and we drove a short distance. She kept looking at a paper with writing on it.

"There it is," she said, parked, and took me with her.

The earthen house had a front yard full of rocks. Ellie rang the doorbell and I heard barking from far away. A lady opened the door and she and Ellie shrieked and hugged like they had each been cooped up at home alone for a long time.

"Oh, my God, it's really you!"

"You look terrific! How many years has it been?"

They continued as we walked in. I sniffed to see where the barking was coming from. The lady opened a back door and three dogs my size came bounding in and jumped all over me! *Outnumbered!* They all sniffed me at once and I couldn't hide. The lady yelled at them.

"Boris, back off and let him alone! Natasha, come this way. Good girl, Katie."

She put Boris in another room, and I visited with the two girls. We sniffed each other, and then they showed me the house and the yard. A man came out of a back room and he and Ellie hugged. The three humans paid no attention to me. They sat and talked and I followed the two dogs around. That yard was one of the strangest I had ever seen. It had no grass! It was all dirt and rocks and those darn prickly plants that had bit me.

After a while, we went back to the hotel, woke Jay up, and we all returned to the house. Suddenly, the humans went out the door, leaving me alone inside with the resident canines! *Help!* How could they leave me unprotected? Boris growled and chased me, so I hid behind the sofa. After a while, he went away and I played with the two girls, but I kept my ears up and my eyes and sniffer sharp to know when I might need to run for cover again. The evening seemed as long as a visit with the vet.

When the people returned, smelling like beans and hot spices, I shook and dashed for the door, eager to return to our safe hotel room and my comfy bed. As I lay there, drifting into sleep, I listened to the sounds of the hotel—people and dogs above us, below us and next to us. I heard their noises: talking, music, feet stomping, an occasional bark or yelp. A machine in the room blew cold air while cars drove by. I was so tired from my doggie encounter, that I slept until morning, without waking up even once.

The next day we were on the road again. We spent another two days with Ellie doing most of the driving. On the last day, I looked out the window and saw low brown hills, leafy trees, houses and fields of vines— familiar territory. We arrived home at dinner time and everyone, including me, breathed a huge sigh of relief. Ellie unpacked the car and made dinner. When we went upstairs, they invited me up on their bed for the night. *Yes!* Traveling is great, but home is the best!

Looking back, I would have appreciated that home-coming even more if I had known it was the last trip we would all take together. I had met new people and dogs and had left my mark all over the southwest, but nothing could be better than being with my own family in the comfort of home. And I had no idea that the next time my humans packed the car for a trip, I wasn't going with them.

FOURTEEN

Hotel Canine

S OMETIMES MY humans pack their suitcases and a big bag of food for me, but they leave my bed at home. It means I'm going to Maria's house, where I will play with my girlfriend Miss Fluffy, run around her yard, and eat her food when no one is looking. Or it could mean I'm going to the doggie hotel. To get there we drive on the highway and turn off onto a narrow winding road that goes uphill to the top of a mountain. Long before the car stops, I smell dogs and hear barking—big dogs, little dogs, yapping dogs, howling dogs, all begging for attention. I figure they all think our car holds their owner coming to take them home to the good life, where they get constant treats and walks and don't have to compete with anyone else. My tail wags a greeting and I wonder who is there.

"Well, hi, Foxy, how are you, boy?"

One of the young men who lives there greets us. My

favorite is Randy, who pets me sometimes—a special treat at the doggie hotel. Ellie talks to Randy while the whole place echoes with barking. I see and smell dogs my size through the glass door to the room next to the entrance. I look for friends from my last visit, and any dog who might boss me around. The dogs in this Pamper Room bark at me, all trying to tell me their stories at once. "Hi, cutie, want to sniff me?" "Come protect me from the bruiser outside!" "Give me some space!" "I'm going to mount you, first chance I get."

Ellie takes off my leash and collar and then she is gone. Randy puts me in the Pamper Room. I meet and greet the others, which takes a while, because there are so many dogs in the pack. They are friendly, but if there's one of those guys with a squashed face, I make a point of growling and chasing him, just so he knows I'm not afraid of his ugly puss!

Every day at the doggie hotel I play with the other dogs, sniff all of their scents, and go in and out as I please through a dog-sized door that leads to the yard. When a new dog arrives, we rush to sniff him. When a dog leaves, we hardly notice, although every time the door opens, we try to escape! When it's time for food, they put me into a small cage, which is OK for a while. I also sleep there. That is the hardest part, because I miss my humans. I hear dog noises all night long—snoring, whimpering, occasional barking or growling. I don't sleep much at the dog hotel and I'm always glad when morning comes. I miss my daily walks and morning snuggles on the bed with my humans.

Then comes the magical day when Ellie picks me up. I'm busy playing with the other dogs, when Randy or someone else invites me to leave the Pamper Room. Then I smell Ellie and see her and get excited. I jump up off the floor and run around her and wag my tail and start my happy dance all over again. Ellie says "sit!" but she doesn't object when I ignore that command—I can tell she is happy to see me too. We go out to the car and I settle down. I sit next to Ellie for a little bit and give her a lick on the face. I stand on my rear legs in the back and look out the window until I see the outlines of home.

I don't know why I have to go to the doggie hotel without my humans. It's one of life's mysteries. But I love them so much after one of these visits. Being without them reminds me how wonderful it is to have all their attention at home. Soon I was going to have more attention than I ever wanted.

FIFTEEN

Fall

AFTER THE hottest time of year, leaves fall from the trees. Walking down the sidewalk when it is covered with dry leaves, I am a powerful brute on the hunt. Crunch, crackle, crunch. I scratch and scrape away the earthy-smelling leaves to uncover something rich and wonderful underneath. If it's especially yummy, I roll around on my back, trying to pick up some of the scent, so I can bring it home and enjoy it again.

When the sidewalks have a blanket of leaves, the air starts to smell of wood smoke and old grapes. The wind blows, ruffling my fur and bringing drops of rain. It takes away recent scents and brings new ones from far away. I hear big birds high overhead, honking to each other as they fly by. I would love to explore all of the smells released by rain, but Ellie hurries me along. When it is raining hard, she puts a coat on me. It covers my head— *hey, I can't hear* —and keeps parts of me from getting soaked. I have no luck trying to shake off the coat. She carries a special stick that opens up into a little roof and keeps some of the rain off, but the wind blows it around so much, I don't know why she bothers. We always do our regular walk, in any kind of weather. Once it was so wet and windy that she slipped and fell. I had to scoot to keep from being crushed by her body or stabbed by her big stick. She got right up and we finished our walk.

After the rain, the street is full of tiny rivers running downhill. In order to cross the street, I may have to jump over the water or walk through it. I become a hunter trying to find my way out of the wilderness. I sniff for wild animals that may be lurking. I move towards an opening in the street that sounds like a waterfall—rumble, rumble—as the water falls down a big hole. I sniff around the opening, wondering what's in there. Oops! Ellie yanks the leash, pulling me away and ending that adventure.

The best part of wet weather is when we get home. Ellie takes off my coat and wraps me up in a warm towel and dries me off, like when I have a bath. Even though I don't like her rubbing my feet, being bundled up makes me feel like a pup again, warm and cozy. When she lets me go, I run around the house, shaking off more water, spreading my wet fur smell, and looking for my favorite toy to beat up.

SIXTEEN

Conehead

WHILE I was trying to figure out what was going on with Jay and Ellie, lots of friends came to visit. One night Gretchen, Mary, and my pal Scruffy stayed until after dark. When they left, Jay went to bed and Ellie took me out for a walk. It was as dark as the time I spent a night behind the laundry in the closet. We were crossing the narrow street around the corner from our house, when Ellie slipped and fell.

Watch out! My first concern was to get out of the way. I scooted aside and the leash dropped from her hand. I had seen Ellie trip or fall before—she always stood up right away and told me, "It's OK," but not this time.

She was lying there in the middle of the street, holding her arm and calling weakly, "Foxy?" I couldn't see much, but a familiar smell told me the neighborhood boys were in the street. As I backed away, they chased me, yelling.

"Foxy, Foxy, come back."

I ran, then sensed movement behind me. There was a loud screech and something pushed me down on the ground.

Ow!

Visions of being hit by a rock in the woods went through my head.

Escape! I ran and ran, then ducked under some bushes and waited until it was quiet. I licked my throbbing leg; it tasted salty and metallic. After a while, I heard someone approach and call my name, so I took off again. The leash dragged behind me and caught on rocks and branches, but I pulled it loose and continued running. I came to a wide divided street. I saw no cars, so ran across. I didn't even pause at the concrete island in the middle. I ran until I was limping and then stopped and looked around.

I sniffed the darkness and shivered, listening to the eerie quiet. I was in front of a house which had no lights inside or out, no car in front, and no sign of humans. My nose detected a slight hint of cat on the walkway and I followed it up to the porch. A cloth next to the door also smelled of cat and felt right, so I curled up and fell asleep. Waking up several times in the darkness, hurting and cold, I wanted to go home, but that would mean crossing the wide street again. I dreamed that Ellie was out looking for me, calling, "Foxeee."

In the morning, I heard sounds in the house and

smelled food. *Pancakes? Eggs?* When the door opened and a lady said, "Hello," I moved toward the smells. Scents of coffee and cinnamon drifted through the door.

"What happened to you, little fella?" she asked.

I answered by hobbling into the warm house. She looked at the jangly stuff on my collar, and put out some water for me. Before I was finished lapping it up, Jay and Ellie came in the door! I was so excited, I forgot that my leg still hurt. Ellie was crying. She picked me up and carried me to the car. Jay drove.

We didn't go home, but to the place out in the countryside that always has humans and pets sitting and waiting: cats, dogs, rabbits. As soon as the car door opened, I picked up the scent of scared animals. Ellie took me past the collection of people and pets, right into a small room and set me down on a table.

"You're such a sweet boy! Dr. Nick is going to fix you up. Be good!"

Dr. Nick was a gentle man with a long coat that had a slight scent of kitty. He definitely had eaten bacon for breakfast.

Bacon, now there's a cheerful thought!

He held something in his hand.

Ouch! What was that?

I slept. I dreamed about searching my yard for lost toys. I was trying to remember where I put the bone with the peanut butter smell when I came to. I was in a cage, like at the shelter, and I couldn't feel my hurt leg. I tried to stand, but whoops, down I went again. The tube sticking out of another leg kept me from moving much. Fur was missing around the tube and the leg itched. Dr. Nick came over and talked to me.

"Hey, Foxy, how are you feeling, boy? I'm going to call your folks and they'll be here soon."

I heard him on the phone talking. Then he opened the cage and removed the tube from my leg.

Yeah! Freedom.

I stepped out and wobbled on my shaky legs. Dr. Nick put a huge plastic cone around my neck.

What's this?

I couldn't lick anything! There was just enough room to get my tongue in the water bowl, but I couldn't get to my leg—or anything more private than that!

Ellie and Jay came to pick me up. I heard something about "stitches" and "two weeks" and "e-collar." I hadn't noticed it earlier, but, just like me, Ellie was not her perky self. One of her arms was wrapped in cloth and she was quiet and did everything with her other arm, so I guessed that she was hurt too.

What a pair we are! I've heard people say that cats have nine lives; it looks like we're giving them a run for their money!

Day after day I struggled with that demon collar. It kept me from doing all of my favorite things: sniffing up close, licking myself, and scratching my ears. Ellie took it off when she fed me. I scarfed down some food, then made a bee line for the bed and dove underneath.

Can't get me here!

I took a nap and licked my paws and then I heard noises in the kitchen that required an investigation, so I trotted out. Ellie walked behind me and closed the door to the bedroom.

Tricked again!

There was that collar in her hands. I backed up down the hall until I had nowhere else to go and she put it on me.

I had to wear the collar on my walks and to bed. It kept bumping things—the wall behind my bed, the floor when I jumped down from the furniture and everything in the car. The only thing it was good for was attention from humans. They all asked about it.

"Oh, poor doggie. What happened to him?"

"Can I give him a treat?"

Treat? Definitely!

Finally the collar stayed off. My leg felt much better. About the same time, Ellie stopped wearing the cloth on her arm, so I guess she was better too. *OK, time to relax.* No chance!

SEVENTEEN

To Bark or Not to Bark

B ARKING IS a unique dog talent. A cat can make noise, but she couldn't bark if she wound herself up in a knot and tried all night. Tiny dogs emit tiny squeaky barks—what an irritating sound. Those dogs seem to be yapping all the time. Big dogs have deep, thundering barks. My bark is just about right—low and masculine, and loud enough to get your attention. I don't bark very often; it is a skill saved for special circumstances.

I have different barks for different reasons. When there's a stranger at the door, I try to sound like a big, mean dog with a low, loud bark or howl. Back when I first joined Jay and Ellie and they left me at home alone, my constant bark of fear and loneliness left me exhausted. When I was learning to walk on the leash, I barked a friendly announcement to dogs on the opposite side of the street. It was a greeting, like "Hi, I'm Foxy, who are you?" combined with "Don't get too close to my side of the street, or else!" When I did this, Jay would yank the leash, but Ellie would tell me to sit and then talk to me like I had done something bad. I couldn't believe she didn't want me to express myself with my throaty announcements. Then I barked in the car when I saw a dog through the window.

"Hey, this is my street, watch out!" I barked. The sound echoed through the car. *Cool!*

Ellie really didn't like that.

"Foxy, knock it off!"

I understood how important this was when she grabbed a bottle as we were on our way out the door for a walk. When I saw a dog and started a low growl, she sprayed me in the nose with water. *Huh? Achoo!* That's how I learned to skip barking on walks and in the car— well, most of the time.

There is one house we pass on our morning walks where I want to bark every day. My ears and nose go up as soon as we get close. I have never seen the dog behind that tall fence, but I can hear his panting and smell his anger. He thrashes his body against the fence. He sounds huge. He growls as soon as we are close, so how can Ellie expect me not to reply?

Ellie makes me sit and tells me to walk *with* her, and I try my best, but I'm so caught up in the waves of energy coming from that guy behind the fence, I just can't help myself. I pull at the leash and dance around on my back legs and bark my heart out until we're past the house. Then I hear all of the dogs in the neighborhood baying too. I like to think they're cheering me on. Maybe one day I'll be brave enough to skip barking at the bruiser behind the fence.

It's not only big, noisy dogs that set my fur on end and my bark in motion; some of the little squeaky ones can be terrors as well. Ellie and Jay have lots of friends who have dogs—Scruffy, Shadow, and then there is Star. Star is teensy tiny, short-haired, and pushy. She wants to be the boss at her house and everywhere else, and she always yaps at me to remind me of that, like I could ever forget! I usually hide under a table or on someone's lap to get away from the little monster. One day Star's human put a new collar on Star. It had a funny lemon smell. I guess Star didn't like it much, because she didn't bark at all that day! I don't know if it was the collar that did it, but it was sure a treat for me!

Although Ellie clearly doesn't want to hear from me when we're out, it's part of my job to bark when someone comes to the front door. As soon as I hear or smell someone outside—long before my humans know—I run to the door and alert everyone with a loud bark. If Jay or Ellie doesn't come right away, I increase the speed and volume and add a howl. They are quick to tell me to stop, but they don't object to this barking. In fact they usually say "good boy" before asking me to cease and desist. Then they open the door and talk to the person who is there. They don't seem to be concerned about these intruders, so I just mind my own business until the visitor leaves.

EIGHTEEN

Party Animal

N OT LONG after our accident, Ellie launched into a flurry of activity and I knew guests were on the horizon. A party is a time for humans to talk, eat and talk some more and requires the whole house to be clean in advance. After the party there is more cleaning and moaning about spots on the rug not made by me. Ellie moved furniture and pushed around a cleaning machine. It made a hot, noisy wind that could knock me off my feet, or worse, suck me up into its dark, musty interior. *Under the bed!*

She swept, polished, and went out, returning with bags of food. *Cheese? Crackers? Salami? For me?* She cooked for hours and then organized everything and put it away, without giving me a thing. *Drat!* Jay spent most of his time on the sofa watching TV. Neither of them paid attention to me, unless I made any kind of mess—then they banished me to another room.

"Foxy, who spilled your water? Foxy, off the sofa. You'll get hair on it!"

The party preparations were familiar, but something was different. When Ellie prepares for guests, she sings along to loud music. I hadn't heard any music or singing for quite some time. Jay slept a lot and talked very little. Whole days passed with no tummy rubs and my walks had become shorter and shorter. I carried Ellie's shoes around the house and occasionally chewed on them. Pretty sad entertainment.

Jay no longer took me for rides in the car. I watched Ellie go into the closet, take the keys out of his pants pocket, and put them in a drawer. One afternoon he went out to the garage and stood by the car, but he couldn't get in. Ellie followed him.

"Jay, sweetheart, you can't drive. It's just not safe."

"I want to go out!"

"I'll take you anywhere, but you can't drive."

Finally party day arrived. Ellie made the table bigger and put all the food out. *What a feast!* Cheese and crackers, grapes and strawberries, chips and dips. It all smelled wonderful, but she didn't drop any on the floor. A taller dog might have jumped up to the table as soon as she left the room, but my legs don't reach that far. I could only drool in anticipation of a future spill.

Ellie swept, washed the backyard and filled it with

chairs and tables. Ellie and Jay changed their clothes in the middle of the day. Then the doorbell started ringing. Party days are a challenge because I want to do my job— barking when the doorbell rings—but I get confused when it rings so often and rather than thanking me for my effort, my humans only shush me.

Once the house filled with people, I visited with the ones I knew and checked the floor for lost morsels of food. People crammed every corner. They milled around inside and out in my yard, eating, drinking, and babbling at each other.

"It's been so long since we've seen you!"

"Beautiful day, huh?"

"Pleased to meet you."

"Jay is so quiet."

"It's the brain tumor. He's really having a tough time now."

Everywhere I turned there were feet of all sizes, some covered up, some showing painted claws. I sniffed the feet of those who were seated, checking for animal smells and hoping for a handout.

"Hey, Foxy!" Miss Fluffy's human, Maria, gave me a hug and a backrub. I wished she had brought Miss Fluffy, but I rolled over and gave her my tummy without hesitation.

"Foxy, the handsome boy!" That was Scruffy's human,

Mary, who had left Scruffy at home. *Drat!* Didn't they know I wanted guests the same height as me?

Jay sat on the sofa all afternoon. He didn't move or speak or look around. People perched next to him and talked and then moved on, but he stayed in a long "sit." Ellie was all over the place—talking to people, moving the food around, opening bottles, filling glasses.

When people began to leave, Jay struggled to get up from the sofa. Very slowly. Someone came over and put out a hand to help him, but he said "No!" in a loud voice. I ran out of the room, tail tucked in, but looked back to see what he was doing. He took a few steps, then slipped and fell, bumping his head on the wall. Everyone jumped up and two men pulled him up from the floor. Ellie ran in from the yard, took his arm, and helped him climb the stairs.

When she came back down, people asked, "Is he OK?"

She said, "He's OK, he's OK, he's OK" over and over again like she does to me when I'm scared.

Soon the guests hugged Ellie and left. It was quiet again. She put the leftover food away. *Drat!* We went up and joined Jay in the sleeping room. Life got back to normal, but Ellie was often up during the night when she should have been asleep, sitting hunched over at the table and staring into space.

Is everything really OK?

NINETEEN

Scratcher

I GIVE my belly, neck and ears a good scratch from time to time. Just like stretching or rubbing my tummy on the rug, it's a great way to greet a new day or just let the world know I'm feeling content. Sometimes I get an itch that won't go away. I scratch and scratch some more, and still I itch.

Ellie looks at me funny when I'm really itchy. She says, "Stop, Foxy." Like I can really not scratch something that prickly? *You try it!* Yes, she scratches herself too. Sometimes my scratching is so bad she gets out that frightful cone collar or she takes me to the doggie doctor.

Once Ellie left me with her friend Carol, who lives with two big humans, a baby and two big dogs. It was hot at their house, but they had a huge backyard with grass for running and bushes and trees for sniffing and peeing. They left the door to the yard open a lot, so the other dogs and I could go out whenever we wanted. *Cool!* The two dogs were easy going and we all shared the space without getting in each other's way.

I looked around after exploring the yard and saw that Ellie was gone. *Sleepover!* I slept on my bed in Carol's room upstairs. She took us on a nice long walk every afternoon in the heat. Loved the walk, hated the heat. It was OK, although I missed my snuggles with Ellie and Jay. And the special treats they drop on the floor when they're having dinner.

At first the itching wasn't a big deal—just a prickling on my rump near my tail. But it didn't go away. Luckily, I could reach the pesky area with my teeth, so worked it around to get a little relief. Then my belly tickled. And my neck. I scratched and scratched and scratched. Soon I had places that still itched, but also hurt and were wet, so I licked at them. Licking made me feel better.

I barely slept, as I itched the most at night. Carol kept waking up and talking to me, but that didn't do any good. I had no interest in food or water. All I wanted was to scratch those itches away.

Finally Carol put me in her car and took me to a doggie doctor. A lady doctor poked me and handled me all over. Her helper held me while she came at me with a metal object that had teeth. Before I could check it out, it started buzzing, and the next thing I knew, fur was flying and I had a bald spot on my butt. The helper put me in a tub and washed me with some bad-smelling stuff. I didn't see how any of this was going to stop the itching. The doctor forced some pills down my throat. Then we went home.

Carol stopped at the store and came back to the car with the dreaded cone collar and put it over my head, adjusting it to fit snugly. *Ooooow!* I couldn't lick my bald spot or scratch my neck! That night I slept a little and the next day Carol fed me from her hand and took me for a nice walk. Then Ellie walked in the door! *Yeah! Take me home.*

Back at my house, Ellie gave me another soothing bath, brushed me, and rubbed my belly. She put some cream on the parts that still itched. One day they left me alone and I figured out how to get out of the collar. I wasn't so itchy anymore, but gave myself a much-needing licking all over. How can a dog stay properly groomed with that damned cone on?

That should be the end of the story, but after we had been home for a while, I started to itch again. I stood in front of Jay and scratched at my belly furiously. *Help!* He stared at me. I continued to scratch, this time my snout, until it hurt.

Ellie put some cream on my snout and went to the telephone. "Poor Foxy, please let it not be fleas again!" She put me in the car and we went to our usual doggie doctor, who took one look and said, "Yep, he's got fleas."

The doctor gave me some big clumps of stuff that tasted like peanut butter. Ellie took me home and brought the cone collar in from the garage. Back in treatment. Finally the itching stopped and my fur grew back on the bald spot. I'd sure like to know what "fleas" are and how an activity as pleasurable as scratching can lead to such misery.

TWENTY

My Leash on Life

I TINGLE from the end of my nose to the tip of my tail when I see my leash, but the leash is no fun when I want to chase a squirrel and Ellie has other ideas. She tugs, snapping the harness, and tells me to hurry with words like: "Let's go," "Come on," "Foxy!" When I find treats in the grass she yells, "Leave it." She pulls on the leash at the same time, so I'm out of luck, unless I'm fast enough to scarf down the yummy stuff before she knows. When we go to the dog park, however, the leash comes off. *Freedom!* I run ahead to scout the trail or stay behind to explore, but when she calls me, I run to her for the joy of her company and some nice words: "Good boy!"

Usually I am only on leash when we are outside or visiting a new place and Ellie wants me to stay near, so I was surprised, soon after our party, when she put the leash on me at home. It wasn't only my itching that had been strange at our house. Jay slept most of the day and didn't play with me. Ellie no longer talked to me all day long and didn't throw my ball or offer tummy rubs. She took me for walks—short walks—and sometimes Patty, our neighbor across the street, took me to the dog park.

Patty used to have a big, friendly dog, but I hadn't seen him in a long time. She also had two cats. After a couple of short visits in her house, I knew those cats were up to no good. They hissed at me and climbed up on the furniture to look down on me. I liked Patty, but I didn't like being in her house for long.

One day, two men came to the door. Ellie invited them in and they went upstairs and with much grunting and sweating, they moved Ellie and Jay's bed down the stairs and put it in front of the TV. Then they moved the sofa and table upstairs. Ellie brought my bed down and put it near theirs. That night Ellie and Jay slept in the living room. I went upstairs to see what was going on, but it just looked like the rooms had been switched, so I went back down to my bed.

Soon after, one night at bedtime, Jay threw up. Ellie crooned, "Poor baby," and got Jay out of the bed, which now had a strong smell. She ordered me out of the way. I heard a siren approach, then a loud motor at our door. I saw flashing lights through the windows and hid in the kitchen. I saw two men lift Jay onto a bed and roll him out of the house. Ellie put the leash on me and walked me across to Patty's. Patty came right to the door. Ellie talked fast and left me there.

I spent the night with Patty and the two monster cats. I might have wondered what was happening to Jay and Ellie, but I was too worried that those cats would jump me while I was asleep. The next morning Ellie brought me home, but Jay wasn't there. She invited me to sleep with her on the bed in the living room. I licked her wet face and nestled in the curve of her legs until we both fell asleep.

A couple of days later Ellie took me in the car to a place where I had never been. A building, bigger than any hotel I'd seen, was surrounded by a parking lot full of cars. She took me in on the leash. There were no other dogs and all of the people coming and going through the big entrance turned to look at me. We rode one of those moving rooms up to a long hall, to a tiny room where we found Jay alone in a tiny bed. Ellie put me on the bed with him, and I sniffed alcohol and blood while he ran his hand up and down my back and relaxed. Strangers came in and out of the room, giving Jay little tablets to eat. They looked like the pills Ellie shoves down my throat sometimes. The strangers talked quietly with Ellie. The place had a serious feel, like when my people are about to take me to the kennel, but they don't want me to know. I think Ellie went to see him every day, because we returned to that same parking lot often. Sometimes she left me in the car and came back just to give me a walk or some water before disappearing back into the building. Sometimes I got to go in and visit Jay.

Ellie continued to sleep downstairs, and was often up during the night. I got used to this, but then the two men returned and moved the bed back upstairs. They brought in a narrow bed and put it in front of the big living room window. Ellie took new sheets out of their wrapper and put them on the bed. A truck rumbled to our door and suddenly there was Jay, carried in on a stretcher and moved to the bed. I was excited to see him and ran up with my tail wagging, but he was sleeping and didn't notice me. When Ellie put me on the bed, I sniffed and licked him, but he didn't pet me.

The house was full of new scents—Jay's medicines and Ellie's heartbreak. Friends and strangers came to visit every day. The house filled with a quiet tension. I was glad that Jay was at home, but he stayed in bed and slept all the time. I missed our life like it used to be— our walks to the coffee shop, trips in the car, sitting on the sofa with Jay on one side and Ellie on the other, both of them petting me. Every night I snuggled next to Ellie and licked her hand while she smoothed my tummy and whispered comforting sounds to me. We wrapped each other in sadness.

After a few days, Ellie took me to the kennel, but I didn't see any suitcases packed. When I came home, after a few more days, everything had changed. The house was full of wilted flowers. Jay was not there and the small bed was gone. Three strangers slept upstairs, two of them in our usual sleeping room. Ellie wanted me to sleep with her in the room that was only for visitors. She scolded me when I hesitated.

"Foxy, get in here now."

The man kept calling my name and wanting to pet me. The two females didn't approach me, but I didn't know them and I wanted to know why they were sleeping in my room on Ellie and Jay's bed. And I wanted to know where Jay was.

After quite a few days, the visitors left, and we went back to sleeping in our room, but I was afraid of what would happen next. Ellie didn't go out or talk much. She didn't do anything with me except take me for short walks, so I kept to myself. If she went up the stairs, I'd go down. When she walked down, I'd go up. If she came after me, I'd hide in the corner or under the table. She blocked the stairs with a gate, like when I was sick and she used the gate to lock me in the kitchen. I don't like that gate. I hadn't done anything wrong!

Then she put the leash on me, so I couldn't get away. Actually that was OK. She'd pull me up on the sofa with her and pet me for a long time and we would both lean back and relax into our warmth. She started spending more time with me and taking me for wonderful long walks. Most nights she invited me to sleep on the bed with her. I missed Jay, but Ellie and I had new ways of being together. Jay never came back.

Once in a while we drive up a narrow road on a hillside, park and walk to a particular spot on the hill. Ellie sits down in the grass and talks to Jay. I know that because I hear her say his name. She usually cries when we're there. I think she's glad I'm with her at the other end of the leash, reminding her that, whatever happened to Jay, she and I still have a connection. Our family has become smaller, but we are still here for each other.

TWENTY-ONE

Winter

WHEN IT is cold and the grass is frosty, Ellie takes a long time to get ready for a walk. She stands in front of the window, takes things out of the closet, puts on shoes and a coat, coverings for her head and her front paws—all that before she moves towards the door. Then she gives me a very serious look. *Watch out!* She puts a tight stretchy sweater over my head and my front legs. It feels so snug on my back and my tummy, I try to shake it off. I still enjoy my walk, but the only time I really appreciate that wooly garment is when the ground is covered with ice.

I've been to places where the ground is frozen, the air is crisp and cold, and Ellie's feet make loud crunching noises as they break through the crust of snow. When we come inside out of the winter's cold, we warm up right away. At our house we have a hole in the wall where Ellie can put some wood and make a fire, but she doesn't do it very often. When we're at a house in a cold place, however, she always makes a fire. It sends a nice smoky smell into the air. I like to lie on a rug nearby, listening to the snapping sounds from the wood and feeling the warmth of the fire on my cold nose. It's a great place for a nap.

TWENTY-TWO

The Big Chill

SOON AFTER we lost Jay, we went to visit our friend Marcie in the woods. I did not see my bed go into the car with Ellie's bags. At least I smelled the bag of kibble, so I wouldn't go hungry!

I looked out the window for a while at passing cars and then curled up and took a nap. We stopped in a shopping center and Ellie left me; she returned smelling like hamburger and fries. *Where's mine?* She let me out for a short walk and offered water, but I wasn't thirsty—just hungry for hamburger!

After more driving, we left the main road and I knew we were getting close when I heard the crunch of tires on rocks and saw dust rise around the car. We went up a hill and around a bend and turned into a driveway. It took us down to a house sitting under tall trees. When the door opened, I heard scrambling squirrels and smelled the night creatures who had left their mark everywhere.

Marcie hugged us both. "Well, hi there Foxy, how are you?" There was a fire going in the stove in the kitchen and everything—even my own fur after a while—smelled like wood smoke. She showed us to the back bedroom.

Wait—there was something weird going on. That smell? Could it be? There was a definite scent of cat coming from the other bedroom. I poked my nose in the doorway and there on the bed was a giant two-toned creature who took one look at me, arched her back and hissed, spraying her spit across the room.

Marcie ran in. "Now Gracie, be nice to Foxy. He's a sweet dog." Gracie was having none of it and slunk under the covers, disappearing. I escaped to the other room and again wondered where my bed was.

After a while it got dark, Marcie's friend Tom came home, and the three humans spent an eternity in the kitchen cooking, talking and drinking wine. I stayed close by, near the warmth of the stove, positioned to keep one eye on the room where the monster cat was hiding. Despite the heat from the stove, the house got colder and colder.

At bedtime we went into the back bedroom. Ellie picked me up and put me on the bed with some murmuring about "Sorry I forgot your bed, Foxy." She crawled under the covers and turned out the light. I tucked my paws in to keep warm and tried to relax. Just as I was about to doze off, there was a bang from above, then a scurrying, scratchy noise from the roof. I sat up, ready to flee. Ellie put her hand on me and tried to soothe me: "It's OK, Foxy. It's just acorns falling on the roof." I did not understand, but knew she was telling me not to worry. I lay down again. Moments later the sounds came again and I sat up. Her hand came out from under the covers. This was going to be an interesting night!

We both fell asleep eventually, but sometime during the night Ellie turned the light on and gave me a funny look. I was shaking. Well it was really cold. Ellie pulled me close to her and tried to put her arm around me. Now I love my human and I love the belly rubs she gives me when we cuddle in the morning, but most of the time I like a certain amount of distance from her heavy arms and her noisy breath. I moved away and continued to shiver. She fell asleep, but later she woke and reached for me. She encircled me with her arm and dragged me under the covers. She made a little cave by holding up the blankets with her arm. She pulled my backside against her chest and held me there. I was not happy, but it was warm in her nest. Somehow we made it through until morning.

We both perked up after our morning walk; the sunshine warmed us. Back in the house I treated myself to a bowl of food I found in the kitchen. That day I went with all the humans in Tom's car into the woods. The car bounced up and down on a dirt road. Ellie held me close on her lap. Too close for comfort again. We finally stopped the car and took a walk in the woods. I smelled lots of wild animals. We stopped at one place with snow on the ground. Marcie held my leash while Ellie took pictures. I took the opportunity to slurp some icy water out of a creek.

Back at the house, I immediately went into Marcie and Tom's bedroom to see what Gracie was up to. She was hiding, but I could smell her. Then Marcie shooed me out of the room. Later I was sitting with the people in front of the TV when Gracie came prowling down the hallway. I started shaking again. *Keep that cat away from me!* Soon it was time for bed and Ellie and I went back to the icy dungeon. Once again the night was filled with alarming noises from above, and Ellie pulling me under the covers.

I never got to meet Gracie the cat. She stayed in the bedroom and Marcie kept me away from her. One evening I went into her room and we stared at each other silently before someone noticed. After several nights that seemed like forever, we finally got in our car and drove home. Back in our warm house, I ran around checking on the health of my toys, drank some water from my own bowl and eyed my bed with longing. That night I walked in circles in my bed, until it was just right for lying down. Safe at home at last.

TWENTY-THREE

Boot Camp for Miss Fluffy

I LOVE Ellie, but it is great to have a special dog friend—
Miss Fluffy. She gazes up at me through soft hair that
hangs down into her eyes. She doesn't seem to mind the
bow Maria puts between her ears. She is smaller than
I am, but walks like a duck, her big belly swinging from
side to side. Her squeaky noises and special smell make
my tail wag. She goes up to every human she sees to sniff,
say hello, and get a pat on the back. *Have you no fear, girl?*

I run to the door as soon as Maria's car pulls into the
driveway. Maria greets me with a back rub and claps her
hands so I'll jump on her. I don't trust many humans, but
Maria is on my short list. First Fluffy goes directly to my
food bowl to see if I've left her anything. When we finish
running all over the house to express our excitement,
we greet each other with the usual sniffing of both ends.
Then we go for a walk with Ellie and Maria; sometimes
we have sleep-overs.

When we're together, I don't miss an opportunity to show Fluffy who's boss: *Hey Fluff, watch me pee on that tree.* She whines to go out, which she needs to do often. Such a wimp! But a sweet-smelling wimp and a buddy who sees things from my perspective—that is, from a foot off the ground. When Miss Fluffy comes into the house, the games start.

"See that rope toy? Let's see who can get it first?" she seems to say, as she races for the toy box. She bites one end and I bite the other, and the tug of war is on. A playmate is a great thing to have, especially when Ellie spends the afternoon sitting in front of that box of flashing lights on her desk. When Fluffy spends the night, she sleeps in her tiny bed, right next to mine.

Mealtimes are a challenge, wherever we are, because Fluffy thinks my kibble is the tastiest thing she ever swallowed and I feel the same about hers. Ellie stands guard in the middle of the room.

"In this corner we have Foxy's food. Stay back, Fluffy! And in this corner, we have Miss Fluffy's food. Uh uh, Foxy!"

As soon as Ellie looks away, I scoot over to Miss Fluffy's dish and scarf some down. Miss Fluffy does the same with mine. In the end, we both get plenty to eat and Ellie has no idea who ate what.

Miss Fluffy and I like to get attention from humans,

but especially when we are together. I can sleep under Ellie's bed all day, but if Ellie is on the sofa scratching Miss Fluffy's ears, I want some too. It works both ways. If I climb up on the sofa for a tummy rub, Miss Fluffy has to get up there too, only she needs Ellie to help her up.

The only problem with Miss Fluffy's overnights is when Ellie walks both of us. I've searched for a polite way to say it—Miss Fluffy, you are a bit overweight and poky—no—you're just plain chubby!

She takes no offense, but, with her nose in the air and her tail wagging, her look tells me she's a lap dog after all, meant to sit on some royal person's knee all day getting frequent caresses and just going out in the yard when it's necessary. I, on the other hand, love my long walks and running in the dog park. When Ellie takes us out, she struggles with the two leashes and Miss Fluffy just hangs back, taking her time, not a care in the world— what a pain! Sometimes she even sits down and looks at Ellie and me as if to say "I'm done!"

One day Ellie announced, "Enough of this! Miss Fluffy, you're going to go for a good walk and exercise off some of that fat!"

Ellie put Miss Fluffy on one of my old, short leashes. Then she hooked it to the side ring on my harness. All of a sudden, we were a parade, with me as the leader! *All right, junior dog, follow me!*

Then Miss Fluffy decided to stop and sniff some grass. I was walking along at a brisk pace until—oof—it was like trying to pull a bag of kibble. I looked at Ellie and she looked at me.

"Let's go, Miss Fluffy," she ordered.

Fluffy glanced around and then started moving again, at first slowly and then picking it up to a decent amble. I stopped to sniff a tree and pee on it and Miss Fluffy trotted ahead of me. *Hey! Cut that out! I'm the leader.*

Ellie untangled the legs and leashes and we started out again. The next time Fluffy did her cute squat to pee on a plant, I waited, then lifted my leg and marked the same spot. Eventually, this system worked pretty well.

Once we took Miss Fluffy to the dog park. Ellie met a friend with a big dog and we all started up the trail together. Ellie had Miss Fluffy on a leash, but the other dog and I were loose and running ahead. *Let's go, Rambo, I'll race you!*

Fluffy poked along dragging the leash way behind Ellie, who called her to catch up. "Come on, Miss Fluffy, you can move faster than that! Come on, girl!" I looked back and saw Miss Fluffy sit down and wag her tail. *All done.* I waited with Ellie's friend while she took Miss Fluffy back to the car. When she returned we finished our long walk in the dog park. Everyone got what they wanted that day!

TWENTY-FOUR

Cavedog

S MALL DARK places call out to me for exploration, and I can't resist. If you ever wonder where I am when you holler and I don't come, I might be in the back corner of the messiest closet, burrowed under a pile of dirty old clothes. I might be under a bed where I've taken all of my toys, to make sure you can't play with them while I'm having a snooze. Or, if you've let me out in the yard, I might be under a bush, or under the deck.

When we moved to our current house, and I first visited the backyard, I found a deck, with dark, moist dirt under it, the perfect place to crawl and explore. I might find a puddle of water there long after it stopped raining, or bugs or poop from other animals available to roll in. The first time Ellie couldn't find me, she came out on the deck and called me and ran all around the yard looking under bushes.

"Foxy, are you out here? Foxy! Foxeeeeeeee!"

I crawled out, tail wagging, to find her standing with her hands on her hips and no smile on her face.

Soon after that, two men came to our house and started taking the deck apart. I had to stay inside for days while they worked outside. Eventually, there was a new wood deck which smelled like a forest. When I finally got to go out and dive underneath, I saw the dirt had been covered with cloth. It was still fun, but Ellie scolded me every time she found me there.

"Foxy, what are you doing under there again? What am I going to do with you?"

Then a man worked in the yard all day nailing something up around the new deck. When he left and Ellie let me outside, she was smiling and standing straight and tall. I saw that the deck opening had been sealed off. Well, almost sealed off. A tree was growing in a corner between the steps and the house. There wasn't enough room for a human to stand there, but a tiny space had been left open under the deck. I crawled under to see what I could see, while Ellie was talking over the fence to the man next door.

"Yeah, Don, I had to have the work done to keep the dog from going under the deck. What a relief that's taken care of now."

I had fun for a while, but then I wanted to get out and I couldn't remember where that opening was. Ellie went in the house, but before long, I heard her calling me, as she had before. "Foxy! Foxy, where are you now?"

She walked in and out of the house, her voice rising into the panic range. I moved around under the deck and cried softly—*Mmmm? Mmmm?*

"Oh no! How did you get under there?" She went to the tiny opening. *Oh! There's the way out!* I went to her and stuck my nose through. I smelled her and wagged my tail, but it took several attempts before I was able to squeeze myself just the right way to crawl out. She put some boards over the opening, but I still find a way under there occasionally.

Once Miss Fluffy went under our deck and Ellie got upset all over again. Miss Fluffy is shorter than I am, but she's pretty fat. She also wasn't clever enough to go to the opening when Ellie called her. Ellie had to put some cheese through that hole to coax Miss Fluffy out! Next time I'm going to hold out for cheese.

On occasion I have to tell Ellie where I am. If I'm out in the yard, I have to wait a long time for her to come and open the door for me. Sometimes I bark to remind her I'm out there. Once at bedtime, she turned out all the lights and I was still sitting on that deck waiting to come in! I barked once and then many times before she came to the door. Once I was inside, she kept saying, "Poor Foxy," and calling me her "little sweetheart." Even though it was late, she got out my dog biscuits and gave me a treat.

Once in a while I don't come when Ellie calls me because I'm snoozing under her bed. She gets down on her four legs and looks underneath. I move my tail to let her know I'm happy to see her, but I'm not ready to come out yet. It's nice to have a space that is only for me—and a safe place to hide when I don't want to do what the humans have planned for me!

TWENTY-FIVE

Bigfoot

SOMETIMES ELLIE leaves me at Miss Fluffy's house for the day. I jump up and squeal to see Fluffy and Maria. Fluff and I run around the house, go out into the yard, play with her toys and take naps together. I have a great time, but I am always happy to see Ellie when she picks me up.

I knew something was different the afternoon when Ellie didn't come, but instead Maria put me in her car and drove me back to my house. Maria didn't ring the bell, but walked right through the door. Ellie was lying on the bed, and one of her paws looked as big as a ham. *I'd love some ham—on the bone, please.*

I got close enough to sniff her, and that paw sure didn't smell like ham! It smelled more like the doggie doctor's office. I couldn't see the foot, because it was covered by a thick wrapping of cloth and clay.

"Hey, how are you doing?" asked Maria.

Ellie answered in a sleepy voice. "I'm OK. The pain hasn't kicked in yet. Just groggy."

When Maria left, Ellie got up to follow her to the door. She stood next to the bed on her good foot and put her knee down on a contraption with wheels and handlebars, like a small bike. Ellie held on and rolled slowly to the door, pushing with her unbandaged foot. Maria laughed and said good-bye, but I jumped out of the way. *Watch my feet! No rolling machines in the house!*

That night, Ellie slept with the scooter by her bed. In the morning, I waited by the front door for my walk. When the doorbell rang, I barked my warning. Ellie lifted her ham-sized foot out of the bed, climbed on her scooter and, while I stayed clear, she went to the door and let in a boy. I had met Alex a few days before, when he and a girl I didn't know went on a walk with us. He held the leash on that walk, but I kept trying to escape.

I'm outa here! But Ellie had already put the leash on me. She handed it to him! I couldn't run back to the bedroom. He opened the door.

"Come on, Foxy. Let's go for a nice walk."

"Go on, Foxy. It's OK." This from Ellie.

No way! He pulled and Ellie pushed, and I ended up outside walking with Alex. I followed the usual trail of smells, but walked as fast as I could, pulling Alex along. I wanted to get home fast. When we got back to the familiar yard and door, I shook all over and wagged my tail. Ellie was waiting for us. I spent the rest of the day under the bed. In the afternoon, I gave her "the look" when I was ready to go out, but she just talked.

"Just wait, buddy. Angela will be here soon." *Huh?* She continued moving around the house on her wheels, bumping into things and sounding angry. "Ouch, I'm going to mess up the new paint! Damn—this is exhausting."

Then the doorbell rang. *Rowl! Rowl! Rooooowl!!*

It was Angela, the girl who had been on the walk with Alex. I ran the other way, but Ellie told me to "sit", and before I knew it the leash was on and Ellie had pushed me out the door with Angela. Yep, I had my afternoon walk with another stranger. Was that how it was going to be? No dog park? No running without the leash?

The next day Alex came in the morning and Angela returned later in the day. When Ellie called me to put the leash on in the afternoon, I hid under the dining table and wouldn't come out, even when she offered treats. No walk for me. Ellie let me out into the yard, or I would have burst.

The next morning, when Alex came, I hid under the bed. He got down on the floor and called to me. "Come on, Foxy, we'll have a fun walk. Come on, I have to go to school." I didn't budge and in a little while he left. Ellie rolled around on that machine grumbling, so I stayed under the bed. I heard her talking to someone.

"Are you the trainer? I'm having a major problem with my dog...yes, that would be great." Soon the doorbell rang and I came out to do my usual howling. The visitor was another stranger, a lady who smelled like turkey and cheese. She sat down on the floor, totally relaxed, and I went over to find the source of those smells, which was her pocket. *Turkey? I'd love some turkey.* She started giving me treats. *Yeah!*

Ellie sat on a chair, and the lady put treats on the bigfoot! I grabbed a piece off the bigfoot and scooted away as fast as I could. That bigfoot was as hard as a rock, with a rough surface. I ate more turkey and cheese off the foot. *My new best friend! Keep the turkey coming!*

The treat lady said, "See, he's getting over his fear already. Do you have any peanut butter?" *Peanut butter?* Ellie rolled to the food room and came back with a jar. *For me?* Although it sticks to my tongue, I love the smell and taste of the stuff. The visitor put her finger in the jar and smeared some onto the metal scooter. *Huh? Is she nuts? Slurp, lap, yippety yay!*

Once the scooter was clean, she put more on! This was my idea of a fun way to spend the morning. The lady put my harness and leash on me. She and Ellie sat and talked and then the visitor left. I still had the leash on when Angela returned to walk me in the afternoon, and Ellie grabbed it before I could hide. Feeling rather satisfied—*hey, I had turkey and peanut butter*—I accepted my afternoon walk with Angela.

After a few days, I didn't mind the scooter so much, or the bigfoot. Ellie kept me on the leash all the time. She spent most of the day on the bed, with her leg on a pillow. Sometimes I jumped up to join her, and sniffed the bigfoot to see if it had changed. Lots of people came to visit. The visitors knocked and then walked right in. *No! Who are you?*

I had fits of barking, growling and howling, then hid from the strangers. I would, however, come out to investigate when they brought food. *Warm apple pie? No thanks. Spaghetti and meatballs? Just drop it on the floor!*

Occasionally a friend came to take Ellie out. One day she returned with a changed foot. It was covered by a boot that she could remove. With the boot off, I saw that her foot was smaller. It still smelled like alcohol and stinky medicine, but it was just a foot.

Before long, Ellie started driving the car, and I got to go along. She rolled to the car, folded the scooter, put it inside, and we were off. Once, Ellie took me for a walk with that scooter. At first, she moved slowly, but then she started rolling pretty fast and I pulled her along. *Cool! Foxy the sled dog!*

One day I watched her put the scooter in a box and take it out to the garage. No more scooter. She walked with a limp for a while, and the kids still walked me sometimes, but soon we were back to our old ways. And finally she took me back to the dog park, where I could run free, without the leash. I loved it more than ever, knowing I have four feet that work really well!

TWENTY-SIX

Timber!

WHEN I first saw my humans drag a tree into the house, I was sure it was a treat for me—my own watering post. Someone said "Uh-uh" every time I approached it, so I learned the tree was not there for my release or entertainment. That was long ago.

Last winter Ellie put that tight sweater on me—ugh—and we rode in the car to a little forest. She picked up a long-handled thing with sharp teeth, and we walked among the trees. I smelled the blanket of dried needles on the ground, the sappy stumps where trees used to be, and the pee spots left by other dogs. It was a fun walk, except she was talking all the time: " How about this one, Foxy? No, it's too short. Maybe this one—no, it has a hole in the side. Maybe this one?"

It continued until she circled around one tree, left it and came back to it again.

"This is it!" she announced, as if she had just spent an

hour digging up a delicious bone. She dropped the leash, told me to "stay" and gave me the look that goes with it. I sniffed around the area while she got down on her knees and sawed away at the tree. She grunted and groaned, paused to take off her coat, then I heard more grunts and groans, along with the "udge, udge" sound of the saw. Finally, she stood up, pushed on the tree and it fell over, releasing a strong piney scent.

Then we went into the little house nearby. It was warm inside and I wanted to take off my sweater, but that was not part of the plan. The place smelled like apples—from a pot of steaming liquid and the cup Ellie sipped from. The people who ran the place talked to me.

"Hi, Foxy, you're looking very Christmassy today!"

"What kind of dog is he?"

"Are you ready to have your picture taken?"

Ellie sat down in a big chair in front of the fireplace and lifted me onto her lap. A lady with a camera made noises; I looked away. Something squeaked and I looked up, ears at attention. Flash! Bright lights blinded me.

Back in the car, I enjoyed the tree scent all the way home. The next thing I knew that tree was standing up in the living room. Ellie collapsed in her chair appearing very satisfied. The next day she put shiny balls all over the tree. For a while I dreamed every night about chasing critters in the piney woods.

TWENTY-SEVEN

A Pooch for All Seasons

AFTER MANY days of the rain and cold, new fresh-smelling grass begins to sprout everywhere. I lick the fresh blades and leave my scent on new places in the yard and at the dog park. Long after the rain stops, I find pungent mud clustered around puddles of water in the park. Some dogs run straight for the mud puddles and jump in. They roll around like they are taking a bath and enjoying it. Then they shake, sending a shower of mud flying far and wide. Their owners laugh or shake their heads.

Ellie tries to keep me out of the muck and that is OK with me. Sometimes there's no way to follow the trail without walking in it. If I get too deliciously dirty, Ellie gives me a bath when we get home.

I enjoy my late afternoon walk when it's warm and sunny and lots of dogs are out for their exercise. All the bushes have new buds and we try to get our pee as high up on the bush as we can to see who is top dog. The breeze is full of new smells. I hear chirping everywhere. The bees are back around blooming flowers. Their buzzing tells me that long, warm days are coming.

Is this my favorite time of year? It's hard to choose. The trees have new leaves fluttering in the breeze and the rose bushes along our walkway are opening. Sometimes Ellie picks me up to smell an especially wonderful bloom that's near her nose. That's one of the times I know how lucky I am, in any season.

TWENTY-EIGHT

People Envy

I'M PROUD of all my doggie talents—things like digging up buried treats, running like the wind, and sniffing the air to know what kind of a day is ahead. Some dogs act like humans exist just to take us for walks and give us food and treats and tummy rubs, but I'm amazed by what you two-legged creatures can do.

Probably the biggest difference between us and you is what comes out of our mouths. Yes, we bark and whine and growl and sigh, but you humans have a constant, ever-changing mix of sounds coming from your lips and it all seems to mean something. I know by Ellie's tone whether she's happy or angry. There are some messages that are directed right at me that tell me what to do, like "sit" and "down" and "wait" and "uh-uh." She talks to me all day long, even though I understand very little— I wag my tail and try to act interested in all of her noises. When she's not talking to me, she often speaks into a little box she holds next to her face. All humans use those little boxes with their strange noises—music, buzzing, dings—during the day and in the middle of the night too. People stop whatever they are doing—like getting my dinner—to pay attention. Very annoying!

When you humans meet, you don't have the courtesy to sniff each other or avoid eye contact. You get very close, look directly into each other's eyes, sometimes touch, and then your mouths start up and talk flies back and forth. It is boring for the poor dog whose walk has been interrupted and who must wait impatiently to sniff what lies ahead on the path.

Humans use teeth for chewing, but unlike us dogs, yours are all about the same size. When you're angry, you don't curl your lips to threaten attack—you're more likely to use a loud voice or throw something. I've learned when to get out of the way. People do something else with their mouths that's very weird. You press them up against each other (or me) and make squeaky noises. This appears to be something soft and tender, like a gentle massage, but it puts me on alert, wondering if a bite is coming. When I see your mouths approaching, I look for a quick escape.

As much as I'm fascinated by how you use your mouths, I think the most wonderful thing about humans is your paws. I wish my back paws were like yours.

How do you stand on those two legs all day and not get really tired? Human back paws smell like yeast and dirt. Ellie paints her claws with something that makes them stinky and shiny. I don't know why she does this, but I've caught her putting on different shoes and admiring her paws in the mirror.

The front paws of humans are even more amazing. Ellie uses hers to do so much—dish up my food, hold the leash, clean the crusty stuff around my eyes, brush me, pet me, put pills down my throat—the list goes on and on. I guess that's what happens when you don't have to walk on paws—they become talented tools. If I had paws like that I could scratch all of my itches, carry more than one toy at a time, clean my teeth when something gets stuck in them, pull out foxtails without help, move my bed or my food bowl whenever I want to—oh the joys of being human! I'd even be able to turn off the TV when I want some quiet!

Another thing Ellie does with those paws—she sits for a long time holding a book. She occasionally puts it in my face so I can sniff its musty paper and glue.

"See my book, Foxy?"

We have several shelves with row upon row of these books, and often packages arrive containing more. She enjoys this activity in the evening. She sits by the light for hours, looks at the paper, and turns the pages. When it is time to sleep and I'd really like it to be dark, she lies in bed with one of those books. She must need the light to see it, because she puts the book down just before she turns off the light and says, "Night night, Foxy."

You humans don't have the common sense to bury what is precious to you. The house is outfitted with spaces for storing things. There are tiny rooms with doors just bursting with cans, cloth, glass, wood, paper, wax, and other stuff. The curious dog eager for a scavenger hunt just needs to wait for a door to be left open.

Our sleeping room has a closet with clothing on hangers. Every day Ellie pulls different things out of the closet and gets dressed. Without these clothes she is pretty funny looking. That's because you guys don't have much hair, except on your heads. Without fur, your skin looks thin and weak. I guess you'd be pretty uncomfortable outside without the clothes, but on a hot day, I don't see why you bother.

At night Ellie takes off her clothes and puts them back in the closet or in a basket. When she takes the basket into the garage, gushing and thumping sounds follow, making me think we have uninvited company. She brings the clothes back out, folded and warm in her basket, with an herbal aroma so strong, it's like nothing in nature. I love to roll around in the smelly clothes and carry them around when I get the chance, but she usually snatches them away before I can play.

On my own I'd have to hunt for food, not knowing whether something would turn up under a bush or I'd still be hungry at the end of the day. Not so for you lucky humans. Ellie gets in the car and drives to a big store. She finds a metal wagon and rolls it into the building. She comes out with her wagon full of bags that she squeezes into the trunk, away from my disappointed nose. I enjoy the ride home while sorting out the aromas of meat, fruit, bread, and vegetables drifting from the back. *Mmmmmm. Maybe a sandwich?* I'd love to have some time alone with those bags, but she is always in a rush to unpack. She puts some things into the refrigerator. *Do I smell cheese?* The rest goes in the closets, and nothing is left for me.

Speaking of cars, I wonder what it would be like if I could drive. When I'm left alone in the car, I like to sit in the driver's seat and pretend I can make the car go. I imagine myself driving to all my favorite places. I'd keep the window down so I could smell everything passing by. If one of my favorite smells came up, like pancakes, for example, I'd just stop the car and get out to investigate. Maybe that wouldn't be such a good idea. I could go from pancakes to hamburgers to fresh cookies and wander off for hours, without remembering where I left the car or how to get home. I guess I've had enough problems from following interesting scents—I'll leave the driving to you talented humans. And hope I get to go along for the ride.

TWENTY-NINE

Suitcase Blues

Eᴸᴸɪᴇ'ꜱ ꜰʀɪᴇɴᴅ Mark used to join us on walks once in a while and sometimes he stayed for dinner. I didn't want to get too close to him—he's a guy. You never know when one of them might want to kick you or hit you with a newspaper. One day he came over and Ellie handed him a bag of treats.

All right! Party time.

Mark got down on the floor. He lay on his back and put the treats all over his body!

Huh? I didn't want to get too close, but those treats were calling me. I approached slowly, grabbed a morsel off his arm and took off. He stayed on the floor, silent. Ellie sounded very excited, saying "Good job, Foxy!" Really—all I did was scarf down a treat. It tasted great. I went back again and snagged one off his leg. Soon all the treats were gone and Mark stood up looking very pleased with himself.

A few days later we played this game again, then Mark took me for a walk without Ellie. *What's going on?*

I got my answer the next time Ellie took the big zippered suitcase out of the closet and placed it on the floor. I was on high alert, because I knew this meant a trip, and if I was lucky, I'd be going too. I sniffed around her feet as she moved back and forth between the closet and the drawers, putting clothes in the suitcase. I nosed around the bag when she left the room, but only got a whiff of the stinky stuff she sprinkles on herself every morning.

The next day, Ellie took me out for a walk so early it was still dark, and then she put that bag in the car. I heard the garage door and the car driving away and I was alone. Left behind again! I went back to sleep. Well, there was nothing else to do—she didn't even put food in my dish! After daylight arrived, the door opened and I hoped that maybe she had come back to get her little buddy. No, it was someone else. The familiar scent of our friend Mark was better than a stranger, but I was confused.

"Hey, Foxy boy," he said. "You're looking well today."

It was just Mark and me. When he tried to put the leash on me, I ran out of the room and down the hall until he cornered me in the bathroom. Leash on, I followed him outside.

Mark let me pee wherever and whenever I wanted. We took long slow walks—not the brisk march that Ellie demanded. Mark slept in the front room and I slept in my room. It was strange to be there without the sounds of Ellie snuffling in her bed. Mark fed me and talked to me and reached out to pet me. I jumped back to avoid his touch, but was always happy to see him come in the door, because it meant I would soon be enjoying the air and smells of the outdoors.

The sight of the suitcase still makes me wonder whether I should pack my toys and my treats, but even when I'm left behind, I know I won't be alone.

THIRTY

The Harshest Sound I've Ever Heard

ELLIE AND I were hanging out in the cool house on a warm spring evening. She lay on the sofa with a book and a box of those lovely paper tissue toys I like to play with. She kept sneezing, kissing those tissues, and leaving wadded up bunches around in piles I couldn't get to. *Darn!*

She was in front of the TV and I was on the floor next to her when I heard the first "BEEEP!" That sound pierced my head like a sharp thorn. I ran out of the room. She got up mumbling something about "damned cell phone," went to her desk, fiddled with the object, sighed, and lumbered back to the sofa.

Two minutes later, "BEEEP!" A clipped, piercing sound—*ouch!* I ran around in circles. She got up again.

"Humph, not the cell phone. Could it be the smoke alarm?" She stood in the hallway looking up at the ceiling.

"BEEEP!"

"I think it's the one in the office," she said and walked to her desk, again looking up.

What's there to see, I wondered. It's a blasted noise! And it's blasting my ears.

"BEEP!" She left the office, closing the door.

She went back to the sofa grumbling. "Not tonight. I just don't have the energy to climb up there—achoo!"

"Beeep!" It was only somewhat muffled, so I had to get out of there. I gave Ellie the "I need to go potty" look. She opened the back door. *Escape!* I ran out into the yard, sniffed around, peed here and there just to celebrate my freedom, and lay down on the grass to relax. I could hear music from over the fence and people talking next door, but no beeping.

Ellie came to the door. "Foxy, come on in."

I looked at her without wagging or moving a muscle. *Near that dogawful noise?*

She came out, picked me up like some kind of baby, and carried me into the house. She set me down and turned to close the door, but quick as a flash, I was already out again. No more of that hauling me like a sack of groceries you can take anywhere you want!

A few minutes later she was back with the leash, crooning to me.

"Sit. Be my good boy, Foxy. Come on now. Sit."

I couldn't help it. She always gets to me when she

tells me I'm good. I sat. She put the leash on and the next thing I knew, with a bit of a tug at the threshold, I was back in the house. She led me to the bedroom opposite the shuttered office with the demon noisemaker. She left me and closed the door.

"Beeep!" Yeah, maybe it was not as loud, but its sharpness still hurt my ears. I didn't like being shut up in the bedroom. I stood by the door, breathing hard, drool trickling out of my mouth onto the floor.

"Beeep!" Ellie came back in with the phone in her hand.

"Hi, Gary, thanks for helping. How do I get the hard-wired smoke alarm to stop chirping? Oh. I don't remember if there's a battery. OK, I'll try. See you tomorrow."

She opened the door and I slipped out, panting and shaking while she brought a little ladder from the garage, went into the office and, with a groan, climbed up on her desk. She fiddled with the disk on the ceiling and climbed down with the thing in her hand.

"OK. Now it's disconnected. That should take care of it."

You know what happened next: "BEEEP!"

"Oh my God," she squeaked as she ran to the kitchen. She pulled things out of the closet and scattered them on the floor while muttering, "Where are those goddamn batteries?"

Finally, having found what she was searching for, she went back to the office and worked more on the alarm.

It was finally silent, but *I* was on full alert, with that sharp sound still echoing in my ears. Ellie shut off the TV and got in her bed. I jumped up, wanting to be close to her. I needed protection, in case the piercing noise returned. I sat and panted. She petted me. I relaxed a little, but didn't go to sleep when she shut off the light. I had to be ready to run.

Much later, she got up in the dark and invited me to go outside. I'd been on the bed for hours, so it seemed like a good idea. I felt safer in the yard. Then she called me to come in. Uh-uh.

"Foxy, where are you?"

I should have known what would happen next. She went back in the house and returned with a light and the leash. Trapped once again, I followed her into the house and curled up in my own bed. As I finally drifted off to sleep, I hoped for quiet dreams, but I kept one ear cocked, just in case.

THIRTY-ONE

Circus Star

I KNEW something was up one night when Ellie filled her pockets with treats and led me to the car. We drove through town to an old building that smelled like a thousand dogs. I was surprised because I hadn't been to dog school for a long time. We walked into the biggest indoor space I had ever seen. Kennels lined one wall, some filled with dogs who were panting and sniffing. People were moving a bunch of equipment from the sides of the room and setting it up in rows on the cement floor. They balanced long bars on top of holders so the bars were my height from the ground. I soon learned those bars were hurdles for us to jump over. They put up fences and some long snaky tunnels. *Really?* And they had ramps that went up and down like the ones I like to pee on at the dog park.

The human in charge was a lady who talked in a load

hoarse voice to all the people, who then lined up with their dogs in different parts of the room. We practiced "sit" and "stay" for a while. Then the leader gave each person a disc and we practiced "touch." This is pretty easy. Ellie put the disc on the floor—actually it looked like the cover to some cottage cheese. She said "touch" over and over and if my nose went to the disc, I'd get a treat. Pretty dumb, really, but I liked the treats, so I learned to do that fast. We practiced "touch" at home before the next class.

We went to this class many times. I got to do a lot of running from one part of the room to the next. I learned when Ellie said "over" to jump over one of those bars. That is if I was aimed right. Sometimes I just walked around it. I was good at running up a ramp on one side and down on the other. When Ellie said "table" she wanted me to jump up on a platform and sit.

The first time Ellie told me to run through the tunnel, I stopped and looked at her. *Huh?* She walked me back and then tried again. "Tunnel," she yelled, as if there was a plate of chicken I needed to scarf down before someone else got to it. I didn't know what she wanted. Finally she sat me down in front of the tunnel, so there was nowhere else to go. I took a few steps inside, then turned around and came out, very happy with myself for solving that problem. She just shook her head. We did some more jumps and ramps and when we came to the tunnel again,

I went all the way in and then stopped. What now? Ellie was yelling, "Come on Foxy, you can do it!" I could hear her huffing and puffing as she ran away from me and I followed her voice through the tunnel until I saw her head in the opening at the end. *Oh, that's the way out!* I ran out and got my treat. I finally knew what tunnels are all about.

The best part of this class was when we did our tricks without the leash. Some of the dogs would run straight across the room the first chance they got, when they were supposed to be running to the table. Then their owners would have to run after them and drag them away from the other dogs, and back to the starting point. Sometimes I couldn't see Ellie or know what she wanted me to do, but most of the time, I did what I was supposed to and got my treat. I even jumped through a hoop, like a circus animal. Yeah I saw that on TV once, but there was no fire around my hoop!

Before the end of the classes, Ellie and I were spending a good part of the night running together as we followed the course from one piece of equipment to the next. She had sweat falling off her and I was panting up a storm, my happy tongue hanging out of my mouth. Halfway through the class, Ellie would take me out to the grass for a pee break. Probably because during one of our first classes, I ran so much I had to relieve myself right there on the floor. After the break, I'd drink a bunch of water.

This class kept us both running. At the end of the night we would drive home, have a snack and we would both go straight to bed.

THIRTY-TWO

Dog's Best Friend

So that's the end of my story, although I don't know what adventures lie ahead. A long time has passed since we lost Jay. It's hard for me to remember him, but we still have some things in the house that have his scent—an old tee shirt and some papers in boxes. Our life is full of fun and laughter, but I still find Ellie sometimes with a downcast face, shedding sorrow. I know when that happens, I can jump up and nestle beside her and give her a lick. When she pets me and talks to me, her sadness dissolves.

Different men come to visit. They talk to me and try to pet me. When they smell friendly, I let them. When we're walking with one of these men, I can do more exploring than usual. The two humans jabber at each other and don't pay much attention to the trail or to me. Back at the house, Ellie cooks and they sit and talk. After dinner, I jump up on the sofa between them to see what happens.

I know it's a good night for Ellie when they both pet me at the same time.

Some humans let their dogs jump all over the furniture, bark at everyone and chase the visitors—including me—and find it adorable. Some dogs want to spend every day filling their bellies, digging holes to bury treasure, or chewing up the furniture. Ellie's look tells when I've made a mistake and she praises me and gives me treats when I'm a good boy. This is much better than being kicked or ignored! I miss Ellie when we are apart. I know she misses me too, because she makes a fuss when she comes home, rubbing me all over and climbing on the bed for a cuddle. She takes care of me and I take care of her.

Some humans use the word "pack" for dogs. They think that even one dog and one human are a pack. Ellie and I aren't a pack—we're a *team*. We look out for each other. When we're walking on trails and she gets ahead of me, she turns and waits or calls me to catch up. When I get ahead, I turn around to see where she is and I wait for her.

When I get foxtails in my fur, she checks me carefully and brushes me to get it all out. Sometimes it hurts, but I know she is doing this to make me feel better. Once I stepped on something that bit me. I yelped and quivered, but Ellie carried me home and put my foot in cool water.

She watched over me until I felt better. Every time she does something for me, I love her all the more. When I give her a lick, the affection comes right back to me. I guess that's what love is all about.

Ellie and I are like family, not like when I was a pup and needed my four-legged Mom for everything, but family in any case. Ellie may not smell as good as a dog or run as fast, but she is mine and I love her. I guess that's what a Best Friend is. I hope that, if I can manage not to get lost again, we'll be together always.

So, dear reader, give that dog nestled by your side a loving caress with your hand. Give him some treats. Take him for a long walk and let him sniff everywhere he pleases. Pay more attention to what interests him. Notice him following your gaze, listening for your voice, adjusting to your moods. Be a friend. Enjoy your canine blessings.

With a lick and a final shake,

Foxy

ACKNOWLEDGMENTS

Foxy owes a huge debt of gratitude to all the human beings who have nurtured him along the way. It's not possible to name all of them, but high on the list are the Friends of the Fairmont Animal Shelter in San Leandro, the Marin Humane Society, and Bridewell Hilltop Kennels in Novato. Veterinarians Nick Morphopoulos, Catherine Cornejo, and Terri Lamp have dealt expertly with accidents, fleas, and disease. Friends and caretakers Debby Wheeler, Maria Laughlin, Womark Kalt, and Trudee Lewis have been able substitutes when I have been away. Foxy loves you all!

The Napa writing community, with outstanding teachers, mentors and productive critique groups, has made publication of this book possible. A partial list of those who helped me put words in Foxy's mouth include Ana Manwaring, Betty Van Patten, Marilyn Campbell, Karen Stern, Lauren Coodley, Pam Jackson, Marianne Lyon, Susan Imboden, and Linda Ellwood. Your encouragement and suggestions have meant more than you

can imagine.

I found Foxy through an online ad that included his picture—how could I resist! If this book has made you want to run out and get a dog, please consider adoption. The internet has made it possible to find the perfect dog. Whether you get a pure breed from a rescue organization or the cute mutt at your local shelter, there are thousands of lost or abandoned dogs waiting for you to take them home and love them. The love you get back makes any amount of needed rehabilitation well worth the effort.

Lenore Hirsch
www.myleashonlife.me
October 2013
Napa, CA

Made in the USA
San Bernardino, CA
18 November 2013